If . . .

YOU ARE A:
- Teacher
- Counselor
- Administrator
- Teacher's Assistant
- Social Worker
- Child Care Worker
- Psychologist
- Pediatrician
- Psychotherapist
- Juvenile Court Worker
- Social Service Case Worker
- Youth Leader
- Religious Educator
- Parent

Who works or lives with one or more
difficult children or adolescents...

Then . . .

This book will help you work successfully,
stay energized and increase the enjoyment you
experience while working with the most
challenging children and adolescents.

Successful Strategies for Working or Living with Difficult Kids

Joyce E. Divinyi, MS

For information, write
The
Wellness
Connection
125 Highgreen Ridge
Peachtree City, GA 30269

Attention Schools & Businesses:
This book is available at quantity discounts with bulk purchase
for educational, business, or sales promotional use.
For information, please turn to the back of the book or contact:
Special Sales Department
The Wellness Connection
125 Highgreen Ridge
Peachtree City, GA 30269

ISBN: 0-9656353-4-1 paperback

Library of Congress Catalog Card Number: 97-91444

COVER, BOOK DESIGN & PRODUCTION BY
ANDERSON IVERSON MARKETING COMMUNICATIONS, INC.
42 EAST MAIN STREET, STATESBORO, GA 30458

WHY THIS BOOK WILL HELP YOU WORK WITH DIFFICULT KIDS

In this book you will learn:

- Why traditional disciplinary methods often backfire with difficult children.

- How to establish conflict prevention conditions within your work setting.

- How voice, body language and creativity can promote or discourage cooperative behavior.

- How to prevent or defuse antagonistic responses.

- How to help impulsive children to think before they act.

- How to communicate effectively with parents of difficult children.

- How to avoid burn out and take care of yourself when working with difficult children.

- Guidelines for working with Attention Deficit Disorder children.

- Ten basic principles for encouraging positive, compliant behavior.

- Guidelines for positive communication with difficult children.

- Crisis intervention strategies for regaining control of an out-of-control situation.

The information in this book has been presented to thousands of professionals working with difficult children in a wide variety of settings. It has been received enthusiastically because it is aimed at meeting the professional's needs as well as the child's needs. The strategies detailed in this book will help you return home at the end of the day with sufficient energy to enjoy your own family.

For the girls and the staff of 'the Home,'
especially Enerys, who taught us all about
"Turning Tragedies into Triumphs."

ACKNOWLEDGMENTS

Three groups of people have my heart felt gratitude for their work and support in making this book possible. The order of their importance to this project is impossible to determine. They all have made an invaluable contribution and without their hands-on work or dedicated support this book would not have been written.

The first are the good, kind and highly skilled mental health professionals who were my mentors, supervisors and colleagues. They taught me much about working effectively with difficult kids and supported both me and the kids with whom I worked. I have had the privilege of working with excellent clinicians and physicians over the years. I especially want to thank David Sorkey for talking me into taking a chance on Enerys, Steve Felker and David Ebron for their generosity and excellent supervision while I worked with abused children at the Home, and Jeff Turley for teaching me about the reality of Attention Deficit Disorder and for convincing me that little boys could be fun, too.

The second group are also good, kind, and highly skilled professionals—but in a different area. My sincerest gratitude to my dear friend Elizabeth Fallon for her labor of love in organization and editing. Diane DeLoach also listened to my ideas and said repeatedly during her years as a single career mom, "You have to write this stuff down." When it came time to do so, I knew I could count on her gift for design and expertise in production to help see the project through. The friendship and professional support of these two women is priceless to me, and Pam Bourland Davis's eye for detail and proper use of language was a boon to us all.

Two other women, Tammy Bjugson and Janice Micallef, who support me on a daily basis, have been and continue to be invaluable members of the team. They are also highly skilled professionals and women who care deeply for wounded children. They are a blessing in my life.

The third group of people are, of course, my family and friends who loved and encouraged me through the course of my professional development. Many thanks to Susan who has been with me since childhood, to Donna, Mary Jane, Cissie, and Sandra whose love is always to be counted on, and to Sandy whose gift of healing taught me to always believe in "Turning Tragedies to Triumphs."

My family is large and deserves to be acknowledged for all their love and encouragement— especially my sister Norma who sat through hours and hours of my classes with patience and enthusiasm. My daughters Bridy and Erin have taught me more than I could ever teach them. Their father Carl, who insists that I got the very best experience with difficult kids simply by living with him for over thirty years, has, in fact, been a gentle loving force for me throughout my entire adult life. Without him this book would not be.

TABLE OF CONTENTS

HOW I LEARNED WHAT I WANT TO SHARE WITH YOU IN THIS BOOK

Shortly after completing my training as a psychotherapist, I was asked to take over the management of a therapeutic group home for adolescent girls who had been removed from their families and were in the legal custody of the state. All the girls had experienced extreme trauma and were often angry, hostile and resistant to most attempts to help them succeed. They were almost always described by teachers, caretakers and parents as defiant, disrespectful or, at the very least, difficult.

While I liked the girls very much, I, too, often found them very difficult to deal with, but I soon came to appreciate three very important facts as I worked with them. First, they are "difficult" for a reason. Their life experiences cause them to view the world and life in a very different way than other children and many of the adults who work with them. Second, because of their different view of life and the world, there are effective and ineffective strategies for working with these children to get them to cooperate and to strive for success. And third, most of us who work with these children do not know effective ways to deal with these kids, and, therefore, usually "react" to their negative behavior rather than **respond** in a constructive manner.

Over and over I have seen well meaning and caring professionals react to these children in ways guaranteed to get the exact opposite response from the ones they were trying to achieve. I became determined to develop new approaches to working with these kids that would not only promote appropriate behavior, but would also encourage them to strive for personal success.

It soon became clear that a new approach did indeed work. The new method was not at all like the authoritarian, punishment-oriented style of discipline which most of us had experienced as children and were trying to use with these kids. I had learned the hard way that the old-fashioned methods just didn't work.

I then became determined to help other professionals working with these kids understand why what they were doing was ineffective and frustrating for all concerned. I wanted to teach the principles and strategies that I knew could get the results they were trying to achieve.

This book is a result of that determination. It outlines an effective, constructive and practical foundation for working with even the most difficult child or adolescent. Since the days of directing the group home, I have both utilized and taught the principles, guidelines and strategies outlined in this book. I have found them to work with children of all ages and to be especially necessary and effective with children who fail to respond to traditional forms of discipline and behavior management programs.

As demanding and stressful as it sometimes is, I greatly enjoy my work with troubled children and teens and often believe that they teach me as much or more than I teach them. I respect their courage and fortitude. They live in a very different world than the one in which I grew up, and I admire their creative, resilient natures which are evident in their struggle to make sense of a sometimes "difficult" world.

These children have a great deal to contribute. It can be wonderfully rewarding to help them achieve their potential. It has been exciting to hear parents, teachers and other professionals say "it works!" when they try a new approach or strategy with a difficult child or teen.

I invite you to consider your own attitudes and assumptions about difficult kids and I challenge you to use the information in this book to expand both your success and enjoyment in working with these children.

What is a "Difficult Kid?"

Most children are considered difficult from time to time, mostly when they are being uncooperative or oppositional. The reasons for their difficult behavior are usually fairly obvious. They are tired, cranky, frightened or maybe just plain stubborn. These children are not normally "difficult," and ordinarily they respond to reason and discipline.

The children I am describing as "difficult kids" in this book do not fit the above description. They are not just uncooperative or stubborn. The reason for their difficult behavior is not always obvious. In fact, it is often perplexing or makes no sense at all.

Their behavior is chronic and often, though not always, is characterized as defiant, disrespectful or belligerent. It is usually self-defeating for the child and frequently results in serious consequences or punishments which rarely change or improve the difficult behavior.

Sometimes the difficult behavior is not angry or defiant but almost the opposite—lethargic, lazy or unmotivated. Nothing seems to work with these children either. They seem not to care about anything.

Both the defiant/disruptive child and the lethargic/unmotivated child or adolescent appear either unable or unwilling to stop the difficult behavior regardless of the repercussions. They do not respond to reason and sometimes seem **committed** to self-defeating behavior. They also seem to be oblivious of other people's feelings. Consequently, they can make you very, very angry. In short, nothing seems to work with these kids.

The sense of frustration, anger and hopelessness that they frequently engender in the adults they encounter sets them apart from their peers. They seem different from other kids and they are. The goal of this book is to explain how and why they are different, and what you can do to get them to cooperate without losing your cool.

Throughout the book, the words "child," "children" and "kids" will be used to refer to adolescents as well as younger children. Often difficult adolescents are emotionally developmentally arrested: below the surface they are young children who have not yet mastered the skills needed to successfully negotiate adolescent developmental tasks.

THE SEEDS OF HOPE

The Seeds of Hope

Anyone who chooses to work with or raise children plants the seeds of hope. Hope for their future, and for yours. Hope for the wisdom and wherewithal to give children what they need to grow into healthy, responsible young adults, and hope, with difficult children especially, for the fortitude to maintain our own balance and health in the process. It takes hope to nurture, train, teach or care for children who often react in opposition or anger to your most dedicated efforts to help them. Planting the seeds of hope can be an exciting and challenging endeavor.

As with any challenge, cultivating the seeds of hope also requires preparation and training. While many people who work with these children have been trained in certain areas, their training is often focused on a single aspect of working with kids, such as education, medical care or social services. Seldom does the training include any of the basic behavior management strategies which make educating, treating or caring for children's needs possible, much less enjoyable. Most parents get no training whatsoever to do the world's most challenging job.

This book is meant to be a training manual. It provides practical guidelines and strategies for meeting this challenge. It is divided into three sections: LAYING THE GROUNDWORK, PLANTING THE SEEDS OF HOPE, and WORKING THE HARVEST.

LAYING THE GROUNDWORK will help you understand how and why it is necessary to change your approach to working with difficult kids. You will be prepared to move from reactions of anger and frustration to a calm but firm response which will help produce the results you seek.

PLANTING THE SEEDS OF HOPE will give you strategies for taking care of yourself while working or caring for difficult children, as well as creative guidelines and instructions for setting up the structure necessary to prevent needless conflicts and power struggles.

In WORKING THE HARVEST you will find simple, easy-to-read instructions for using specific strategies, choosing the BEST strategy, developing a crisis management plan for the classroom, working effectively with parents of difficult children, and most importantly, enhancing and replenishing your personal energy supply.

Each section will give you specific instructions in teaching children the three basic concepts underlying successful and appropriate behavior: SELF-CONTROL, COOPERATION and COURTESY. For children to be successful, both in school and out, they must **first** learn these basic concepts.

- They have to be able to CONTROL themselves in order to learn anything, and they have to learn a great deal in order to succeed.

- They have to be able to COOPERATE in order to work within a system, whether it be a school or the work place.

- Finally, they have to learn the basics of common COURTESY because courtesy is the ability to recognize that other people have rights, too.

Teaching these skills to difficult children is the foundation of successful behavior management training. It is my hope that this manual will help you meet the challenge of working or living with difficult kids.

LAYING THE GROUNDWORK
Can Judgments Get in the Way of Success?

The most troublesome aspect of making judgments and assumptions about difficult children is that we often do not know the whole story of the child's life including all the factors influencing the child's negative behavior. Without that information, we are very likely to misjudge. Never was this so true as with a girl named Jennifer....

HOW DO WE JUDGE CHILDREN?

Most of us have a tendency to make judgments, often without realizing we are doing it. This is particularly true when working with difficult children. Frequently these children stimulate strong emotional reactions, everything from rage to despair. These reactions, in turn, lead us to make certain assumptions and predictions regarding their character and potential for success. I have talked with many professionals who tell me that they know the second day they work with a child that the child is going to be a problem and will most likely create problems for everyone working with them.

Just as our emotional reactions to these children lead to judgments, our judgments have a significant impact on our expectations for these children. And children respond to our expectations. If we believe they are trouble, and will continue to be trouble, often they are.

We even devise elaborate labeling systems to help us define our expectations for these children. Every school system I work with seems to have a lengthy list of labels for troubled, difficult or low functioning children. Sometimes these labels are useful in getting children necessary help, but all too often the labels serve to limit possibilities, creativity and expectations. They cause us to give up unnecessarily or respond inappropriately.

I saw this happen often with the girls of the group home with whom I worked. Frequently, they were labeled "trouble makers," "losers" or at the least, "low achievers." Usually they were treated accordingly. As you might imagine, this engendered anger and resentment in the girls who struggled to believe in themselves when so many had already given up on them. But most of all, it limited the possibilities for success for both them and the professionals working with them. The first step, therefore, in working effectively with difficult children is to suspend your judgments. You can always go back to them. *Start with the idea that this child has the potential for success at some level, and that with creativity, perseverance and the right structure, you just may be the one to help him or her succeed.* You will then have the great pleasure of sharing in their success.

JENNIFER'S STORY

Jennifer was a twelve-year-old girl who had been removed from her home by the state and placed in the group home I spoke of earlier. She was a beautiful child and could be absolutely charming when she was getting everything she wanted the way she wanted it. What she did not want was to go to school.

As a student at the local middle school she soon became known as the ultimate difficult child. She screamed, cursed, cried or carried on at every turn. The teachers, counselor and principal of the school tried to plead, cajole and even intimidate her into proper behavior. This only served to intensify Jennifer's defiant and disruptive behavior. Nothing seemed to work. No matter how angry anyone got with her, Jennifer could, and did, get angrier.

Eventually, it was decided that she would be given a homebound teacher. The visiting teacher was sent to the group home to work with her one on one. The next day the teacher called and said she would not come back. Jennifer was impossible.

Not long after this incident, the decision was made to transfer Jennifer to another facility which had an on-campus teacher trained to work with very difficult children. While we waited for the transfer to take place, I was concerned about the weekend coming up and leaving Jennifer with the houseparents since she had become more and more oppositional and defiant each day.

On Friday afternoon, I decided to negotiate with Jennifer. I told her that I'd excuse her from all chores and group activities so long as she was in her room drawing pictures for me when these activities were going on. My goal was to keep Jennifer out of trouble and away from the other girls, and I knew she liked to draw. In fact, her artistic talent was one of her strengths. She liked the idea of drawing instead of working and agreed to the bargain.

Negotiation was a practical strategy for working with Jennifer. She was greatly pained and anxious about being away from her family. Even though she had experienced severe trauma at their hands, she had always felt responsible for them and was terribly frightened she would never see them again. Her pain was so profound and her anger so great that any approach that even hinted at force or intimidation only enraged her further. The combination of gentle negotiation and structure helped her focus on her strengths and remain reasonably calm for a couple of days — a great achievement for Jennifer.

The pictures on the following page were waiting for me on Monday morning. The bargain held and Jennifer had not been any trouble to anyone that weekend. *The pictures speak for themselves.*

Jennifer's Pictures

"Am I ever gona get away from all the horrible rules? Will it change? Will it change?

"I carry everything (the world) on my shoulders. My problems and other persons problems to."

Jennifer's Pictures

"I feel so crowded."

"Broken so many times and only one little spot for me. and that soon will be covered up with another broken peice."

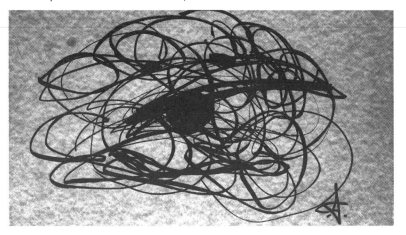

Jennifer and children like her require much of the professionals working with them. The first and second of these many requirements is compassion and an open mind.

SOME OF THE WAYS WE JUDGE CHILDREN

Judgements may include making assumptions relative to factors ranging from "how they dress" to their "ethnicity." Beware of your judgements. They can get in the way of your success.

🍎 How they dress

We can make erroneous assumptions about how a child is dressed. Some splendidly dressed children are very emotionally needy, while some children who look tattered and torn can be full of ambition and intellectual curiosity.

🍎 Personal hygiene

The personal hygiene of a child can be an indicator of the caring and nurturing a child is receiving, but is **not** an indicator of the child's potential for success.

🍎 Family structure or family history

It is easy to make assumptions about a child based on what we know of the family with whom they live, yet children from very stable traditional families can be as challenging to deal with as those being raised in single parent families or by grandparents.

🍎 Intellectual capacity

IQ is only one indicator of learning capacity, yet it is often seen as the definitive predictor of success. Judgments about IQ can impede your creativity in working with difficult children. They can also limit your expectations regarding the child's creativity. IQ is not necessarily an indicator of creativity.

🍎 Level of maturity

Frequently children are judged to be "immature" when, in fact, they are developmentally arrested (See *COULD THIS CHILD BE DEVELOPMENTALLY ARRESTED?*). Both immaturity and developmental arrest can be effectively addressed if negative judgments don't get in the way.

🍎 Ethnic group/race

In a multi-racial culture, it is easy to be swayed by stereotypes. Beware of your assumptions about race and ethnicity. Ask yourself if they may be influencing your expectations for the children you work with.

Personality type

Most people enjoy some personality types better than others. Know your preferences and beware of your judgments about children with personalities that may be irritating to you.

Coping style.

Some children cope with stress, trauma, fear or pain by quiet withdrawal. Others react to the same stressors with anger or agitation or even aggressive behavior. Negative judgments about coping strategies can stand in the way of teaching a new coping skill.

AN OVERVIEW OF THE "FORCES" IMPACTING TODAY'S CHILDREN

One of the most significant ways we judge difficult children is by comparing them to ourselves and the way we remember ourselves as children. And, of course, we always remember ourselves in the most glowing terms.

Have you heard yourself or your colleagues saying something similar to these statements?

"Why are there so many kids like this?"
"What is wrong with these kids?!"
"In my day we would never...."

You are not alone. It isn't just your school or community or workplace. Unquestionably there **are** more difficult children with more severe problems than ever before.

Many believe that the problem lies in the fact that those of us working with these children are simply not expecting as much from them as was expected of us. The above statement, "In my day...," can be heard almost anywhere adults are trying to teach, treat, train or care for today's children.

Unfortunately, it isn't quite that simple. Today's children live in a very different world from the one in which most adults grew up. The differences are profound and are having a serious and mostly negative impact on these children.

When I was growing up, children were very protected from the adult world. In my family, sometimes the children didn't even eat with the adults. We knew that our parents knew everything, or at the very least, they knew lots of stuff we didn't. There was a very definite line between the children's world and the adult's world, and the adults were the vigilant guardians of that line.

Not so any more. *Today's children have been robbed of an age of innocence.* They are exposed on a daily basis to situations and circumstances that most adults never imagined until long after they became adults.

Essentially today's children have been unprotected or **overexposed**. They have been overexposed to many negative forces which rob them of their innocence and leave them feeling or sensing that they are **NOT SAFE**. Safety, remember, is the most basic emotional necessity for all human beings.

Humans are developmental beings. In fact, we have the longest period of development from infancy to adulthood of any animal on earth. Human children are dependent on adults for care and safety during the developmental period. Just as a photograph that has been overexposed does not develop properly into a clear picture, children who are overexposed to negative forces often do not develop properly.

Children must feel safe if they are to develop properly and achieve their highest potential. When they feel unsafe, they act out. Then adults get mad at them, even though the adults have often failed to provide the needed sense of safety.

Consider for a moment the following ways the children you work with may suffer from overexposure. *Today's children may be overexposed to:*

🍎 Adult situations and information

Either through real life circumstances or through the media, children are frequently faced with adult situations which require the most mature mental and emotional capacities to process and understand. Many children spend a great deal of their lives (especially in the summer months) in front of the television. Consequently, they are exposed to every imaginable, and unimaginable, aspect of human behavior, all while they are unable to make mature judgments about what they see.

🍎 Conflicting messages and values

Values and morals which used to be passed down by family and community members are now presented to children through the media as well. This means that children are exposed to many different ideas of right, wrong, good and bad. Exposure to multiple value systems can be enriching for adults, but confusing and perplexing to children, leaving them to try to figure out these powerful issues on their own.

🍎 Trauma and loss.

More children than ever have experienced the loss of a parent through death or divorce. Even in the best circumstances, divorces can leave children feeling many confusing and upsetting emotions. More children than not are living in non-traditional families. They have experienced the pain of the loss of a much-loved parent in their daily lives or, in worse cases, they have experienced severe trauma as one parent makes the decision to divorce an abusive spouse.

Many other forms of trauma affect children's lives as can be seen by the rising incidence of child abuse and adolescent suicide.

🍎 Violence and brutality

Today's children can turn on the television at any hour of the day or night and witness acts of violence and brutality. These programs are paid for by advertisers because research has shown that hearing and seeing a message presented strongly and repeatedly will influence the viewer to go out and buy the product.

Does it not follow that repeated exposure to violence and brutality will also influence behavior? Many who say "In my day..." fail to take this into account, nor do they remember that many of us grew up without ever witnessing violence or brutality in our own homes or through the media. I grew up watching programs like Howdy Doody, and Hop-Along Cassidy was the most violent program I ever watched as a child.

🍎 Passive Activity

Passive activity may sound like a contradiction in terms but it is a good way to describe television viewing. Many children are being overexposed to passive activity because they spend most of their free time in front of a television. It is not just the **content** of television programming that can have an impact on their lives. Even though television programming has certainly changed from the days of Hop-Along Cassidy and Howdy Doody, there are still some excellent programs available for children and adolescents—but there are many things children can never experience or learn by passively watching. The following is a list of activities, skills or character traits that children cannot develop while watching television:

- How to play

- How to imagine

- How to problem solve

- How to communicate

- How to handle their emotions

- How to think

- How to develop a skill
- How to overcome mistakes
- How to set goals
- How to compete
- How to work
- How to interact with others
- How to respond to authority
- How to discern right from wrong

❧ Life-altering or life-threatening decisions

Even elementary school children are being faced with choices about drug use and sexual activity, both of which can be life destroying. How dreadful to have to make life and death decisions without the benefit of maturity, wisdom or experience. Many who say "In my day..." never faced such frightening choices in their day.

❧ Negative and disrespectful adults

Today's children are often hard put to find positive adult role models. Children without positive role models in their families are especially vulnerable. Even at the highest levels of our society, adults can be seen and heard (again via the media) to speak and act disrespectfully and without honor. *Children have always been witnesses to bad adult behavior, but never on the scale they now experience.*

❧ Noise and stimulation

We live in a very noisy world. We think nothing of the lack of silence, or of peace and quiet. Children are exposed to constant stimulation. Some spend the vast majority of their lives in front of the media. They have little time to think, imagine and daydream. All this is done for them through the media.

❧ Environmental toxins

While every effort is made to protect children from environmental toxins, today's children are growing up in a world environmentally very different from the one in which their parents and grandparents lived as children. It is easy to forget that whatever toxins are present in the environment, they impact children more than they do adults simply because of size. How this phenomenon influences the behavior of children is still unknown.

Here again, those who say "In my day..." probably did not grow up in a "day" when their parents even heard of environmental toxins much less had to be concerned about them.

WHY DOES OVEREXPOSURE MATTER?

The results of overexposure to any or all of the above factors can have a powerful effect on children. It can leave them traumatized without anyone realizing they have been exposed to trauma. Exposure to trauma can, in turn, have a profound effect on their behavior and their ability to function successfully.

To work effectively with these children it helps to recognize the signs and symptoms of trauma.

Exposure to trauma can have a profound effect on their behavior and their ability to function successfully.

32

INTERIOR LANDSCAPES
A Behavioral Profile of the "Difficult Child"

ost of the choices we make in dealing with difficult children are based on our assumptions about how they see the world and their place in it, and about how they view authority and authority figures. Usually we assume that their view is the same as, or at least similar to, our own. That is why we find ourselves saying "In my day...," because we assume that if we just treated these children the way we were treated, all would be well. Unfortunately, this is not the case.

INTERIOR LANDSCAPES is a summary and a description of how difficult children view the world and how they react or behave as a consequence of their experience of the world.

Children who have been overexposed to trauma and violence develop deep sensitivities to any perception of threat or force.

DIFFICULT CHILDREN:
Have no concept of future

Future is an abstract concept and many difficult children are unable to think abstractly. Often they are unable to tell you what they want to be or do when they grow up except in the most fantastical terms. They can't conceptualize themselves at a different age or time in their lives. The here and now is all that is real to them.

This presents numerous problems when it comes to educating and disciplining these children because the entire educational system is based on the concept of future, and most traditional discipline methods are based on the ability to perceive future consequences for here-and-now behavior.

Have no internalized behavior management skills

Self-control is a learned skill. It is taught by providing appropriate and consistent external controls throughout the development of the child. Teaching self-control skills takes time, attention and consistency. Many families have little time for this very important process, and our media-driven culture with its emphasis on violence and conflict doesn't provide much support. Consequently, many children are deficient in this very important skill.

🍎 Have poor impulse control

Impulse control is a consequence of training and maturation. When children are developmentally arrested, they are very apt to act without thinking, as is to be expected from infants or extremely young children. People working with these children often do not realize they are developmentally arrested and therefore expect them to have the internal controls they simply don't possess.

🍎 Appear indifferent to traditional discipline methods

Most traditional discipline methods rely on the child's ability to cognitively project into the future. They have to be able to think, "If I do that, I will get into trouble, and I don't want to get into trouble." Without an ability to conceive of the future (even a short term future) or an ability to control impulses, traditional forms of discipline are likely to be ineffective.

To tell children who exist only in the here and now that they are going to get a zero if they don't do their homework, is a waste of time and creates more frustration for the teacher than it does for the students. If difficult children could adequately conceive of the future, the high school dropout rate would not be what it is.

🍎 Have an extremely negative reaction to threat or use of force

Well-meaning professionals working with difficult children often try to appear forceful, thinking to frighten the child into compliance. This frequently backfires with difficult children.

Children who have been overexposed to trauma and violence develop deep sensitivities to any perception of threat or force. Threatening words or gestures or even threats of dire consequences will often cause these children to "feel" as though they are engaged in mortal combat. Their reactions are intense and usually involve inappropriate anger, violence or an extremely defensive shutdown or "stonewall" reaction.

Many difficult children are deeply depressed and experience a sense of hopelessness and despair a great deal of the time. Threat of punishment or censure is irrelevant in the face of despair.

❧ Appear to "space out" easily

This behavior is related to the disassociative process many children living in traumatic and painful circumstances use as a coping mechanism. They don't always choose to space out. It just happens when they feel stressed or threatened. Forceful efforts to get them to "snap out of it" will also backfire.

❧ Are unable to articulate feelings or thoughts

Developmental arrest can affect language processing skills and leave children with inadequate or inappropriate communication skills. It is quite a sophisticated process to be able to identify and articulate the feelings and thoughts that prompt our behavior. Many mature adults are unable to do it.

Professionals working with difficult children often mistake their silences in the face of stressful situations as a reluctance to trust or tell anyone their true thoughts or feelings. Sometimes this is true, but more often, they simply *cannot identify their own feelings much less explain them to someone else.*

❧ Stay either physically agitated or completely lethargic all the time.

Some children are **unable** to relax. They are physically prepared for "fight or flight" at all times. They experience a constant sense of impending danger, usually at an unconscious level. The perceived threat of danger can also cause children to become emotionally "flat" and physically immobilized.

Other children are unable to be still for physiological reasons they cannot always control. It is not always possible to tell from observation alone the reason for a child's physical agitation.

The Impact of Trauma on Children

Many difficult children have experienced great trauma which has a significant impact on their emotional, psychological functioning and, in turn, on their behavior. Understanding how trauma affects behavior can help you deal more effectively with difficult children.

The first studies of trauma came as a result of war in response to soldiers who were clearly suffering from the effects of wartime situations. The studies revealed a greater understanding of what happens psychologically and emotionally to people when they experience severe trauma.

Keep in mind that many children encounter trauma regularly, either first hand or vicariously through overexposure to the media.

The following is a brief explanation of the emotional and psychological effects of trauma.

Disassociation

When trauma occurs, the mind finds a way to help the individual get through it, and it does this by disconnecting the mental processes from the emotional pain, horror or terror of the event. It is a perfectly natural human trait to disconnect mentally from what is going on at the moment. Mostly we call this distraction or daydreaming. Disassociation is the same phenomenon, only taken to the extreme.

Usually people don't even realize this is happening. They don't **decide** to disassociate. They just do it. Sometimes, in the case of chronic or extremely severe trauma, the disassociative process becomes habitual and gets triggered any time the person is feeling stressed or threatened in any way.

As a survival mechanism, disassociation works well. In normal circumstances, it can be problematic because it prevents the normal thinking/feeling interaction that is necessary for good decision making to take place.

Inappropriate Reaction

When the thinking and feeling components of a person do not interact properly, it can cause the person to become highly reactive to even minor irritation or stimuli. Often the reactions do not fit the situations they are facing.

No doubt you have witnessed this happening with the difficult children in your care. When this happens they are usually reacting to feelings they are not aware of and therefore can't process intellectually.

🍎 Hypersensitivity

This inability of the emotions and intellect to interact properly also causes extreme sensitivity to many things that would not necessarily bother people who are aware of their emotions and able to think through them.

With traumatized children, it isn't always emotional stimuli that causes hypersensitivity. It can be things like light, noise, touch, tone of voice, colors, closed in places, or anything that may unconsciously remind them of previous trauma.

🍎 Ineffective Cognitive Processing

When feelings and thinking do not interact, then good decision making doesn't happen. When these two processes are separated, people either do not know what they are thinking or they do not know what they are feeling, or both. Therefore, they act on impulse, which is usually emotionally driven, rather than making decisions and taking action based on a cognitive process.

Difficult children often have this experience. Adults ask, "What were you thinking?!" after a negative occurrence, and children shrug and say "I don't know." Sometimes the response is merely a shrug. Either way, these children are telling the truth. They don't know what they are thinking, or more accurately, they don't know what they **were** thinking when they chose a particular course of action.

They **can** think. They just can't always think at the moment they are feeling an intense emotion. This disability leaves them vulnerable to serious mistakes in judgment and can even leave them trying to figure out why they did something they really didn't want to do.

Imagine how frustrating and troublesome it would be for you if you could not think clearly or effectively any time you were upset. Usually we do not do our best thinking when we're upset, but in order to function successfully in the world, we have to be able to think at least reasonably well when we are upset.*

When feelings and thinking do not interact, then good decision making doesn't happen

* *Further discussion of how to teach children to think when they are emotionally aroused is covered in GUIDELINES FOR WORKING WITH DIFFICULT CHILDREN.*

To illustrate this point, think of the last time you were angry or irritated at your boss. Maybe you felt like saying all kinds of things you **knew** would not be in your best interests. Regardless of the state of your emotions, you were probably able to think about the consequences of being jobless and make a good decision about what you were going to say or do. Traumatized children can't do that.

COULD THIS DIFFICULT CHILD BE DEVELOPMENTALLY ARRESTED?

*A*nother consequence of trauma is that it causes developmental arrest. Humans are developmental beings. They change and grow in their capabilities, both physically and emotionally, from the day of their birth. Notice what babies do when they feel tired, scared, angry, frustrated or unhappy in any way. They cry.

Hopefully, by the time children reach adulthood they have broadened their repertoire of responses to these emotions and can appropriately articulate their feelings. They aren't limited just to crying. This process takes most of childhood and adolescence and sometimes beyond. During that time they slowly change their ways of coping.

Since children are customarily grouped by age in schools and most other settings that deal with children in large numbers, there is usually an expectation that children in a specific age range will function intellectually and emotionally in a similar fashion. Usually they do.

However, when a child has been traumatized, his or her normal development will likely arrest at the point of the trauma. The developmental arrest is further complicated by the fact that as they grow and mature physically, they are expected to behave as though the developmental arrest has not occurred. Teachers, caretakers, even parents don't realize that the child simply has not advanced emotionally and all concerned become frustrated.

There are three specific areas in which this developmental process is most noticeable in children. The first is how they handle frustration, the second is how they problem solve, and the third is how they interact with their peers.

QUESTIONS TO ASK ABOUT DEVELOPMENTAL ARREST

One of the first steps in working with difficult children is to observe their interactions in certain areas. *Ask yourself the following questions:*

- How do their interactions compare with their healthiest peers?

- Have you found yourself saying, "This child is so immature"?

- Do their interactions remind you of a much younger child?

- Do they have difficulty relating to their peers?

- Do they seem unaware that their peers are having difficulty relating to them?
- Are other signs of trauma present?

Once you make a determination that a child may be developmentally arrested (definitive testing can be quite expensive or unavailable), you can then plan your strategies and interventions for the child based on the developmental age you suspect. This strategy alone can alleviate a good deal of frustration for both you and the child.

An example of this can be found in Jennifer's Story. She had experienced extreme trauma in early childhood and tended to react in all the ways mentioned above as a toddler or preschool child would. She cried. She cried if any exchange with the other girls did not go her way. She cried if she was angry, and she cried if she was frustrated or confronted with a problem of any sort.

Her emotional development was clearly arrested. When I looked for an effective intervention to keep her out of trouble with the house parents and the other girls over the weekend, I had to do something much like I would have done with a small child. Distracting small children is usually much more effective than threatening them with punishment or lecturing them about good behavior. Negotiating with Jennifer to draw pictures instead of participating with the group was a way to distract her. It worked. Not only did she stay out of trouble, she left a legacy of powerful pictures of the inner world of a wounded child.

Once you make a determination that a child may be developmentally arrested, you can then plan your strategies and interventions for the child based on the developmental age you suspect. This strategy alone can alleviate a good deal of frustration for both you and the child.

Planting the Seeds

- The Most Important Strategy of All
- Personal Power Tools for Working with Difficult Kids
- Principles for Working with Difficult Kids
- Guidelines for Working with Difficult Kids
- The F-T-A Problem Solving Method
- Understanding Your Own Feelings
- Remember to Keep it S-I-M-P-L-E

The Most Important Strategy of All

Nothing drains your natural energy supply more than the time, tension and effort you give to issues in your life over which you have absolutely no control.

Now that we have outlined why there are so many more difficult children than ever before and why they react negatively to traditional behavior management methods, it is time to look at what it takes to work successfully with these kids. And top on that list is **personal energy.**

Working with difficult kids takes enormous fortitude. When your personal energy supply is depleted, your effectiveness will diminish. If you want to enjoy your work and avoid unproductive encounters with difficult kids, it is essential to keep your energy levels up. Rest, relaxation, personal pleasure and joy are energy building and we will discuss these further in the last chapter, REMEMBER TO L-A-U-G-H. Energy building is important but recognizing what *drains* your vitality is equally important.

Nothing drains your natural energy supply more than the time, tension and effort you give to issues in your life over which you have absolutely no control. It is vitally important to recognize the troublesome and frustrating issues over which we have no control. We spend our time fretting about these problems, not realizing that we are depleting our energies and leaving ourselves too tired to act on the issues over which we **do** have some influence or control.

The ENERGY SUPPLY CHART on the next page is an energy conservation tool. Take a little time to think about the issues and concerns that occupy your daily thoughts. Determine where they would fit into the circles.

- Can you do anything about the situation?
- Can you perhaps influence the situation?
- Do you have any real control of the situation?

Be careful if too many of your answers fall into the two outer circles because the further away from the center of the chart you move, the more your energy supply will be consumed. The arrows indicate depletion of energy.

One of the most distressing things about working with difficult kids is that their needs are usually so much greater than you are able to meet. You can't change the circumstances of their lives, their personal history or their environment, yet we often spend great amounts of energy fretting about these issues.

Stay aware of what you can control. You can control how you interact with difficult children. Usually you can control the environment you create for them and the quality of the relationship you have with them. These areas of control or influence can have a lasting and powerful effect on the lives of difficult children. *Staying focused on your circles of control and influence will also have a lasting effect on your personal health and energy supply.*

Energy Supply Chart

Look at the Energy Supply Chart regularly. Keep yourself focused on what you can and cannot control. Protect your energy supply!

I Have No Control

I Can Influence

I Can Control

Personal Power Tools for Working with Difficult Kids

ou have many personal resources which you bring to your work with children and to which you perhaps have not given a great deal of attention. These resources are your Personal Power Tools. Before you consider strategies for working with difficult children, give some attention to these tools.

Like any tools, if they are to be useful, they must be cared for and used correctly. Taking care of your Power Tools will not only increase your success in your work, but will also make it a great deal more enjoyable.

Personal Power Tool #1:
Individual Energy Supply

Nothing is more important to your work with difficult kids than your personal energy supply. No doubt you have noticed how much more difficult these children can be on the days when you are tired or feeling drained or down. Somehow they have an intuitive sense of knowing when you feel depleted and often react by acting out more than usual.

To respond effectively to the high energy levels of these children, it is essential that you become aware of your personal energy supply and make a commitment to protect yourself from feeling depleted. Everyone has days when he or she feels more energized than others, but it is important for you to begin to think of your energy supply as your most valuable resource. Later in the book you will find more on how to protect your energy supply and how to re-energize when you are tired.

Personal Power Tool # 2:
Attitude

Nothing is as important to personal energy as a positive attitude. By the same token, nothing is so energy draining as a negative attitude.

Yet maintaining a positive attitude can be extremely challenging because you are often faced with situations and challenges beyond your control to change. You find yourself thinking, "If only I could..." knowing full well you can't. This can lead to frustration and a sense of helplessness that translates into a pervasive negative attitude and a serious energy depletion.

Your attitude can become a vital personal power tool when you recognize that it is *the one thing over which you do have control.* Recognizing your freedom to choose your response to any challenge or difficulty enables you to *focus on the power you have rather than the power you do not have.* It is the recognition of this power that has enabled prisoners of war and victims of all forms of tragedy and trauma to triumph over enormous adversity. You can choose your attitude. No one and nothing can control it but you. Beware of energy draining negativity. Let your attitude work for you. It is a powerful tool.

Personal Power Tool # 3:
BODY LANGUAGE

Body language can be an expression of attitude. It can say "Leave me alone," "I'm angry," "I'm scared," or "I'm in charge"—all without a spoken word.

Become aware of your body language any time you are dealing with a difficult child. Make certain it does not attempt to intimidate (leaning over a seated child), threaten (pointing fingers) or disparage (sneering facial expressions).

Body language is a power tool when it expresses confidence (squared shoulders, weight evenly distributed on each foot), openness (arms loose and hands at your sides) and authority (serious facial expression, not smiling, but not angry or threatening). Body language is ever present. Make it work for you.

Personal Power Tool # 4:
VOICE

Have you noticed what your voice does when you are in the midst of a frustrating episode with a difficult child? Does it go up? If it does, you are in danger of sending a message that says "I'm out of control" or "I'm losing it" or worse yet, "I don't know what to do with you." *Difficult children need to know you are in charge and know what you are doing.*

Try lowering your voice the next time you feel like yelling. A firm, low voice lets kids know you mean business and you are in control of the situation. It lets them know that you, not them are in charge.

The tone of your voice, as well as the volume at which you speak, sends an important message. Be certain it is the message you intend to send.

Try lowering your voice the next time you feel like yelling. A firm, low voice lets kids know you mean business and you are in control of the situation.

Personal Power Tool # 5:
A SENSE OF HUMOR

More can be accomplished with difficult children by using friendly humor than almost any other form of communication. Humor, carefully used, sends a couple very important messages. The first is that you and the child are **not** adversaries and the second is that you are certain enough of your authority that you can afford to be playful. Keep in mind that to express your authority is not to be authoritarian.

Authoritarian leaders do not use humor. Confident, authoritative leaders do. Let your own personal style of humor become a power tool for you. Even gentle teasing, if children know you like them, can encourage positive behavior. Have fun. Be playful. Think of humor as your personal power tool and enjoy yourself.

Personal Power Tool # 6:
CREATIVITY

Hand in hand with humor, creativity is an essential power tool for working with difficult children. These children are highly resistant to traditional forms of discipline. Let yourself be creative in searching for both rewards and consequences which will impact these children. Sometimes what may seem like an insignificant reward, like being allowed to lead the class in some activity, may prove more useful in getting a child to comply with behavior standards than an infinite number of traditional disciplinary actions.

Creativity is a problem-solving tool that allows you to try new and different strategies. It will help you to focus on a child's interests and strengths and not just on what is wrong with this child and to use his or her interests and strengths to encourage him or her to behave properly.

Difficult children are themselves quite creative. Allow yourself to think creatively when you are planning your strategies. You may be surprised what works.

Personal Power Tool # 7:
POSITIVE EXPECTATIONS

Mostly we get what we expect. Never is this more true than in working with difficult children. The problem is that without realizing it we begin to expect the worst from these children. Sometimes the systems we work in are predisposed to label children; new teachers and care givers are told in advance of meeting a child to expect the worst.

These children are prone to respond to our expectations. It is most effective to affirm the child's ability to make good choices and to comply with the rules and expected standards of behavior. Note, what you are affirming is *not* that these kids **will** make good choices but that you have confidence that they **can** make good choices.

Affirming your confidence in their ability to make good choices keeps you out of the adversarial role. Since they often enjoy conflicting with teachers and care givers, it is in everyone's best interests for you to refuse to play the conflict game. You can do that by keeping your expectations of the child's **capabilities** high and communicating those expectations to the child as often as possible.

Personal Power Tool # 8:
POSITIVE RELATIONSHIPS

Even the most difficult child has a tendency to get along better and be more cooperative with some adults than others. It may be that one teacher will say "I never have any trouble with him," or a grandparent or some other relative will say "She always behaves for me." It isn't just the disciplinary strategies that these adults use that make the difference with a difficult child. Very often it is the quality of the relationship.

Think of the people in your life whom you know like and think well of you, and then think of how much you are willing to do to keep their good opinion of you. The same principle works with difficult children and adolescents. Even though they can be down-right obnoxious and hard to like, they are usually willing to work hard to keep the good opinion of someone they believe **genuinely** likes them and believes in them.

Building positive relationships with kids requires seeing all their uniqueness and potential, and letting them know you believe in them. It doesn't work to fake it either. These kids **know** who is real and who isn't.

All positive relationships take time and effort to develop. Often adults are so focused on getting compliant behavior from difficult kids that they forget that the kids are people in great need of what Carl Rogers called "unconditional positive regard."

Affirming your confidence in their ability to make good choices keeps you out of the adversarial role.

47

PRINCIPLES FOR WORKING WITH DIFFICULT KIDS

Before discussing specific strategies for working with difficult kids, consider the following fundamental principles which will help you remain calm, effective and energized.

Principle # 1:
CHOOSE A RESPONSE, PREVENT A REACTION.

A strategy, by definition, is a **chosen response**. Planning an effective response **before** difficult behavior occurs will prevent an ineffective reaction. Being well prepared with a repertoire of effective behavior management strategies will help you avoid anger, frustration or discouragement.

Anger, frustration and discouragement are energy draining. It is also energy draining when nothing you try with a child seems to work. Effective strategies conserve energy and encourage positive behavior.

Principle # 2:
YOU CANNOT FORCE A CHILD TO BEHAVE.

Difficult children are immune to attempts to force them into compliant behavior. They are impervious to punishment and are often keenly aware of the limitations of your power to **make** them do anything they do not want to do.

An effective response must, therefore, focus the child's attention on the choices he or she is making and the consequences of those choices. This is not always as simple as it sounds.

Principle # 3:
BEHAVIOR IS A CONSEQUENCE OF FEELINGS AND NEEDS. ADDRESS THE FEELINGS AND NEEDS OR THE BEHAVIOR WILL NOT CHANGE.

Feelings are indicators of needs. Most difficult behavior is a reaction to feelings and thus to needs that are not being met. Children are rarely aware of their feelings or needs, but if their difficult behaviors are repetitive, then the only effective strategies are ones that address the children's needs.

Principle # 4:

IF THE STRATEGY YOU CHOOSE DOES NOT TEACH A SKILL IT WILL NOT BE EFFECTIVE.

Most difficult children are extremely limited in the skills needed to make good choices for themselves. Therefore, if your response to their behavior is not designed to **teach** a skill, it will not be effective. The fundamental meaning of discipline is teaching. Make sure your strategies are oriented to instruction.

Principle # 5:

TELL THEM WHAT YOU WANT THEM TO DO, NOT JUST WHAT YOU DO NOT WANT THEM TO DO.

Positive behavior is necessary to accomplish the goals of a teaching environment or to maintain safety and order in a childcare environment. Children need to be told both the **what and why** of the behavior standards you expect.

Make certain that your standards of behavior are explicit. Explain and discuss exactly what kind of behavior you expect and why it is important for everyone to **cooperate** with these standards.

Principle # 6:

IF THE BEHAVIOR IS UNACCEPTABLE IN THE WORKPLACE, MAKE IT UNACCEPTABLE IN THE CLASSROOM.

Teachers and childcare workers must prepare children for the day when they will have to make a living for themselves. Making a living requires more than a good education or technical skill. It requires the ability to behave properly in the workplace and to get along with employers and other workers.

Children need to be taught the self-control and interpersonal communication standards that are expected in the workplace. *If a behavior would get someone fired in the workplace, it should not be tolerated in the classroom.* If you do not equip children with the skills to get along with people they do not like or in situations they do not enjoy, then they will be unprepared for the reality of the everyday work world where everyone must work with or for people they do not like, or must perform work they do not enjoy from time to time.

Principle # 7:

THEY DO NOT HAVE TO LIKE IT.

An effective strategy does not have to have the approval of the child.

They do not have to like the response you choose to their behavior, or the choices that you outline for them. They must be free to **feel** whatever they are feeling. They simply cannot be permitted to **do** whatever they want.

Principle # 8:

THEY DO NOT HAVE TO LIKE YOU.

While it is important to develop a good rapport with these children, it is not necessary for them to like you all the time. Respectful behavior on everybody's part is essential but does not require that everyone likes each other all the time.

Principle # 9:

IF YOU WANT RESPECT, BE RESPECTFUL.

The **only** way to elicit respectful behavior from chronically difficult kids is to model respectful behavior. You cannot use a tone of voice, words or gestures you do not want directed toward you.

These children neither understand nor embrace the principle of **adult privilege** which was a standard for many of us when we were growing up. Their world is vastly different from ours: it will never again be like it was when an adult's word was law, and adults commanded respect because they were adults.

Now you must both teach and model the behavior wanted from children. If you want children to treat you respectfully, treat them respectfully.

Principle # 10:

IF YOU KEEP DOING WHAT YOU ARE DOING, YOU WILL KEEP GETTING THE SAME RESULTS.

Changing anyone's behavior, including our own is challenging. Responding to difficult children differently than we are accustomed to can feel strange and uncomfortable for a time, **but** the difficult children in your care are not motivated to change their behavior. If anything is going to change, it has to be you.

The same reactions on your part will continue to get the same reactions on their part. While changing from reaction to response and choosing your responses carefully may feel uncomfortable at first, the end result will be greatly rewarded.

These children neither understand nor embrace the principle of adult privilege which was a standard for many of us when we were growing up.

GUIDELINES FOR WORKING WITH DIFFICULT KIDS

Children with "Interior Landscapes" like those described on page 31 can challenge the patience, composure and creativity of even the most sanguine individual. Keeping a difficult situation from becoming a disaster can sometimes be the primary objective when working with difficult kids. These guidelines are provided to help you stay on course when working with difficult kids.

Guideline # 1:

KEEP YOUR COOL.

I confess that the times I have made the most distressing mistakes in dealing with a difficult child or adolescent occurred when my personal energy supply was low. Generally one of two things happens when energy levels drop. You either overreact (usually in anger), or you give in when you know that holding the line is essential for success.

One time, for example, I had worked with a couple of girls for almost a year and had seen outstanding progress in both girls. They both had wonderful, innate gifts and potential for success. Both were, however, still at risk of dropping out of school, getting in trouble with the law or getting pregnant because of their life experiences and traumas. They had been doing well in our program, but this particular day they had gotten in trouble at school, and I was angry with them.

The discussion I had with them to outline the consequences of their negative behavior went very badly. The girls reacted to my anger with an even greater anger of their own. Then it became a power struggle as they tried to prove they had more power than I did. In a way, you could say I won that battle because the girls did experience severe consequences for their acting out behavior; however, my relationship with them was permanently damaged. They believed that I only saw the worst in them and had lost sight of the positive changes they had made in their lives. My anger had caused me to react much more severely than necessary, and I ended up losing their trust. I regret that incident deeply because it had taken a long time to gain that trust in the first place, and as a consequence of my behavior, their positive progress in our program was stopped.

I learned some painful lessons that day. The first is that trust is difficult and fragile for troubled kids. Once it is gone, it can be impossible to get back. Second, they will strive for their own success if they trust you, and they will revert to self-destructive behaviors if they don't. They also become self-destructive if they believe you really don't care about them.

Strange as it sounds, sometimes when kids can't find a way to express their hurt or anger with you, they will opt for self-destructive behavior. It's as though they think, "If I can't hurt you, I'll hurt me." Sometimes they'll lash out at innocent third parties and do something mean or destructive to them. They are usually unconscious of their emotions and consequently are simply acting out feelings that they don't even realize they have. Once they choose a self-defeating or destructive path, it is an enormous challenge to get them turned around.

The third and most important thing I learned that day was that I lost my temper because I was tired. Too tired. I now know that nothing is more damaging to my effectiveness when working with difficult kids than to allow my personal energy supply to become depleted. *I have found that it is unrealistic to expect myself never to get angry when working with difficult, disrespectful, or defiant children or adolescents.* When my energy supply is adequate, however, I am able to maintain my composure and let go of the anger almost immediately. When I'm too tired, my anger ends up influencing my judgment.

That is why the Number One guideline for working with difficult kids is Keep Your Cool! *The following are suggestions to help regain your composure once your anger has been triggered:*

🍎 Take some deep breaths.

As simple as this sounds, the fact is, changing your breathing can change your thinking. Give yourself a minute to breathe deeply **before** you respond to negative behavior.

🍎 Tell the child you are too angry to discuss the problem now and when you will discuss it.

When you are very angry, it is always wise to deal with the issue later. Do not let any more time go by than necessary, but do not hesitate to give yourself time to plan an effective response rather than indulge in an immediate reaction.

🍎 Say your feelings in the form of an "I" message.

Tell the child how you feel. Say "I feel furious when you _____ and I want you to _____." Be sure to include a description of the behavior you want. It is extremely important to model appropriate angry behavior. Many children have never witnessed proper and effective angry behavior. There are far too many opportunities for them to see destructive, aggressive or inappropriate venting of angry feelings.

Also, remind the child of the choices he or she has. "You can sit down now and we will let this go, or if you continue, you will have to leave the room and go to _____ (the principal's office, time out, your room)"

🍎 Remind yourself that the goal of the child's behavior may be to make you angry.

Sometimes you can instantly defuse your own anger when you remind yourself that the child or adolescent is deliberately provoking you. Say to yourself, "Oh no you don't. You aren't going to get to me." Often difficult kids will say or do something to make you angry just to take the heat off themselves and their behavior. If they can pick a fight with you, then the issue will become the conflict between the two of you instead of their inappropriate or negative behavior. This is called "creating a diversion," and children and adolescents are especially very good at it.

🍎 Lower your voice.

If, by chance, you find yourself yelling, stop. Lowering your voice can serve to lower your temperature as well.

Guideline #2:

REMEMBER, WHEN FEELINGS ARE INTENSE, THINKING IS IMPAIRED. WALK THEM THROUGH THE THINKING PROCESS.

Difficult children frequently act on impulse. This is absolutely true when they are emotionally aroused. None of us do our best thinking when we are upset or angry, but difficult children **do not think at all** when they are

If they can pick a fight with you, then the issue will become the conflict between the two of you instead of their inappropriate or negative behavior.

Walking them
through the
thinking process
is different
than telling
them what
they should
be thinking.

stressed. *You can help them engage their own thinking processes by walking them through the thinking process.* Essentially you think **with** them. This is **not** telling them what to think but saying the words you want them to be saying to themselves if they were able to think clearly.

One teacher used this method effectively with a student who was refusing to cooperate and was continuing to disrupt the class. He knew that the girl was very agitated because of a conflict she had earlier that morning with her mother. Instead of threatening to send her out of the room and to the office, he sat down beside her and said very calmly, "Look, this is what's happening. In a few minutes I will have to send you to the office if you aren't able to settle down and do your work. Now, when you get to the office they will call your mother (he knew this to be true) and you have already had a bad time with your mother once today. If you can be quiet and start on your work, you can stay here and not have to deal with your mother again until you get home tonight. If you can't cooperate, you'll have to deal with her again now. It is your choice." The student was able to settle down and get to work.

Simply threatening to send the girl to the office with a statement such as "If you don't settle down immediately, you are going to the principal's office" would have only been an invitation for the girl to keep on acting out and would have forced him to keep his word and send her out of the room. When he walked her through the thinking process of what it would mean if she had to go to the office as opposed to how it would be if she settled down, she was able to make a thoughtful decision as opposed to acting on impulse.

Walking them through the thinking process is different than telling them what they should be thinking. It leads them through a thoughtful consideration of what they are doing, what their choices are, and what could happen depending on the choices they make. This can work even when you are trying to defuse a potentially volatile situation. To say "Calm down!" to someone who is extremely agitated often serves to make them even angrier. If, on the other hand, you say "It's OK to back off now" or even "You can cool down now," you can help them engage their own thinking process. In one case, you are giving a command which may invite defiance; in the other, you are saying words you want them to be saying to themselves. It is the difference between giving someone directions and saying, "Here, let me show you."

Ask yourself what do you want the child to think? For instance, do you want them to think, "If I keep doing this, I'm going to get in trouble"? If so, say, "You can keep doing what you're doing, but if you do, you will _____(describe what could happen)." Outline their choices with them. Remember that threatening these children does not work as a deterrent to misbehavior.

It merely invites more trouble. This may seem like a fine distinction but it is a very important one and can make all the difference in a child's response.

Guideline #3:

BE AUTHORITATIVE BUT NOT AUTHORITARIAN.

An authoritarian approach says, "Because I say so, and nothing matters here but what I say." An authoritative approach says, "Everyone here is important but I'm in charge." Tell the children you work with that you take your job seriously, whether you are a parent, teacher, counselor or whatever, and you plan to get the job done. Establish your authority by virtue of your knowledge, experience and commitment, **not** just because you're an adult.

Children who live in a world that makes no distinction between the world of adults and the world of children (see, AN OVERVIEW OF THE "FORCES" IMPACTING TODAY'S CHILDREN) do not respond to authority simply because the person trying to command is an adult. They have seen too many adults behave badly. Whether or not we think they should, they do resent any approach that puts them in what they consider a "one down" position.

Many of us working with children grew up with authoritarian adults and see this as the proper approach to take with children. It does not work with today's children, and more importantly, it isn't necessary to maintain order and discipline. Be firm and respectful but not threatening. *Remember that threats have a rebound effect on these children,* and put the one making the threats under severe pressure to follow through at all cost.

Guideline #4:

CREATE FUTURE FOR THEM.

Let the children in your care know that you can imagine them succeeding and want to be part of their support team. Remember, they can't

Threats have a rebound effect on these children.

When you
create future
for them,
you help
them see
how good
decisions
produce good
results.

imagine their future. Many cannot conceive of tomorrow or a few hours from now. They are very here- and- now oriented and are seriously impaired in their ability to project their thinking into the future in any way. This is one reason why they are so heedless of the negative consequences of their behavior.

Talk to them about the future. Let them know how the current situation and their behavior will impact their future both in the short term and the long range. Notice in the example given above how the teacher created future for the girl whose behavior was so out of line that she was in danger of serious, unpleasant consequences. He created future for her by painting a picture of what it would be like for her if she would cooperate. Up to that point, the girl was acting on sheer impulse. The teacher not only walked her through the thinking process, but also created future for her.

Be careful **not** to predict a negative future. Do not say, "If you keep this up, you are going to fail." Say instead, "You're too smart to fail. If you decide to work hard at this, you will pass. I hope you do because I think you will like 8th grade better than 7th," or "If you cooperate right now, you'll get to spend time with your computer games at the end of the day like we discussed," instead of "If you don't behave now, you won't ever get to play computer games." These children are acutely aware of the negatives in their lives. They don't need to be reminded of how to make things go badly for themselves. When you create future for them, you help them see how good decisions produce good results.

Guideline # 5:

AFFIRM THEIR ABILITY TO MAKE GOOD CHOICES.

Difficult children are accustomed to hearing criticism. You may have even observed that they seem almost immune to it. At the very least, they don't take it to heart and try to correct their behavior accordingly. What they are **not** accustomed to is hearing that they have the ability to make good choices. They don't even think of their behavior in terms of making choices. Most often, they act on emotion and impulse.

The goal with difficult children is to teach them that when they do something, almost anything actually, they are making a choice, and they have the ability to make a good choice. *It is especially helpful to affirm their ability to make a good choice when they are very agitated and most apt to do something wrong.* You can say, "You're a smart person. You can make a good choice now" in the place of saying, "You better not do that!" or "If you do that, I'll...." It may sound simple but try it. You'll be surprised the difference it can make.

Another way to reinforce their ability to make good choices (which is to say cooperate or behave properly) is to point out when they do make a good choice. Sometimes you can do this when they are expecting a lecture or criticism.

One time this worked well for me after a sixteen-year-old girl and I had an extremely intense and hostile encounter. I had told her we would have to discuss it later when I had cooled down. Subsequently, I went to her room to talk about the incident. She was still quite upset and apparently wanted to show me that she was much tougher than I was. She proceeded to tell me that she "liked to cut people." She had, in fact, lived on the streets for some time, but I chose not to be diverted to another issue, which is what I thought she was trying to do by making veiled threats.

Instead, I brought the conversation around to the incident that had occurred earlier that day. She then said in as threatening a tone as she could muster, "You don't know how lucky you are that I didn't throw that thing at you" referring to a wet rag that she had been holding when she and I came into conflict. I calmly replied, "No, you don't know how lucky *you* are that you didn't throw that thing at me. You made a very good decision because if you had thrown that at me, I would have had to send you to the Youth Detention Center which would have made it impossible for you to get back to your grandmother's house. This way you still have a chance to get your grandmother to take you back into her house (which I knew the girl desperately wanted) and so you made a good choice for yourself. Not only that, you proved that you **can** make good choices and I expect that you will keep making good choices so that you can get what you want for yourself in the future."

She was confused at this point, but also a little pleased because she had just heard a compliment from someone she had set out to intimidate. Even as good as intimidation felt to her, receiving sincere praise felt better. One of the things she had learned early and was no doubt reinforced while she was living on the streets was to defend herself with

One of the things she had learned early and was no doubt reinforced while she was living on the streets was to defend herself with aggression.

aggression. I wanted to reinforce that she wasn't on the streets any more and show her another way to resolve a conflict. We then had a good discussion about why her behavior earlier that day was unacceptable and what acceptable behavior would have been in that situation.

This encounter turned out well in that it did not escalate, and it gave me an opportunity to connect with this girl in a positive way. Let me say that it would not have turned out well if I had not taken time to cool down. Having cooled down first, I was able to create future for this girl as well as affirm her ability to make good choices. It also gave me a chance to let the girl know where she stood with me which is the next guideline for dealing with difficult kids.

Guideline # 6:

LET THEM KNOW WHERE THEY STAND.

A sense of safety and predictability is essential if you want to work effectively with difficult kids. It helps them relax and focus on the task at hand. You can help create this sense by making sure all the limits and boundaries are clearly defined. They need to know exactly what is expected of them at all times and what the consequences of both good and bad behavior will be **before** it occurs.

Without clearly defined expectations, they will constantly be looking for the line. In other words, *they'll look for trouble just to find out where the limits are.* They don't want to "accidently" get in trouble even though there are times they will try to convince you this is what has happened.

Guideline # 7:

BE CALM AND CONSISTENT.

Staying calm means more than not losing your cool. It means staying composed and collected when you are dealing with disrespectful, disruptive or defiant behavior. This can be extremely difficult when your energy supplies are low. Low energy and frazzled nerves lead to inconsistent responses. Inconsistency reinforces the very behavior that you are trying to eliminate.

It is essential that anything that is not ok today **will not** be ok tomorrow or some other time. You cannot maintain the limits and boundaries for

Inconsistency reinforces the very behavior that you are trying to eliminate.

behavior according to your mood. Therefore, it is best not to set up consequences or try to make other important decisions and changes that you are not certain you can maintain and follow through with when you are tired.

Consistency creates predictability, a critical factor in working effectively with difficult kids. If you become unpredictable, they will not trust you, and if they do not trust you, they will not cooperate!

[The section called REMEMBER TO KEEP IT S-I-M-P-L-E explains how to set clear limits, boundaries and consequences **before** problems occur.]

Guideline # 8:

DISTINGUISH BETWEEN THE PERSON AND THE BEHAVIOR.

One of the reasons I was able to compliment the girl in the example above, even in the midst of a confrontation with her, was because I was careful to distinguish between her behavior and her personhood. Difficult kids are used to people not liking them. It is so easy to assume that a child who is always in trouble, or causing trouble is a "bad" kid, a "mean" kid, a "loser" or any number of other derogatory descriptive terms we use.

If you can begin to separate the negative behavior from the true character and potential of the child, you will free yourself up to expect positive changes when it looks like a positive change is impossible. You can let them know that you like them but will not tolerate rude, disruptive or defiant behavior. You can say to them, "I like you but I don't like the way you behave, and I will not tolerate your negative behavior. I think you can do better than that."

Guideline #9:

AFFIRM THEIR STRENGTHS.

One of the most powerful skills you can develop when working with difficult kids, is the ability to identify and affirm their strengths. *Keep in mind that the flip side of negative behavior is often an indicator of character strength.* For example, the child who somehow manages to command the attention of the entire class no matter how hard you try to keep him or her under control, has powerful energy as well as an innate ability to influence others. Many political leaders, public speakers and teachers have this same strength.

The opposite is equally true. Maybe you have almost given up on a child who always seems to be in his or her own little world, detached and uninvolved with whatever is going on with the group. From the perspective of strengths, these children have an inherent ability to detach that may be impossible to teach another child. They have the potential to be excellent rescue workers, emergency room professionals or firefighters. They have a natural ability to keep their cool in the face of enormous pressure (in this case you).

When you see the positive possibilities of a child's negative behavior, you can acknowledge and affirm their strengths with them and then help redirect their negative behavior into positive outlets for the same trait. For example you can say to a child, "You are a smart person; you will make a good leader someday. Let's decide how you can lead the class or group in a positive way." Then set up a structure that will make it possible for the child to do just that **after** they have been cooperative. Kids who are attention seeking, love it when you give them a chance to be leaders, but they have to be taught how to use their talents positively.

The F-T-A Problem Solving Method

F-T-A: Feel-Think-Act

Difficult kids need to be taught to understand how feelings and thinking interact and that they **can** think **before** they act. *Of all the things we try to teach children in school, rarely do we teach them to understand their own emotions and behavior.* This is sad and foolish. We do attempt to teach them something about how their bodies work. We consider it a necessary part of a comprehensive education for a child to know the basics of human biology, but we do not consider it necessary or important for them to understand the basics of human psychology or the dynamics of human behavior. Apparently we assume that intelligent people, children and adults alike, automatically know this information.

The fact is that the tendency toward impulsive and self-defeating behavior has nothing to do with intelligence level. Extremely bright children, and adults for that matter, can and do act impulsively; they may have the capacity to think and problem solve in certain situations and still be unable to deal with their own emotions or interact effectively at an emotional level.

In fact, the more intelligent difficult children are, the more frustrated people working with them become. The tendency is to expect basic intelligence to translate to positive academic performance, and cooperative and acceptable behavior in the classroom and elsewhere. Yet, it is common to find children with high scores on standardized tests failing academically and getting into trouble for disruptive and uncooperative behavior.

The problem is their emotions govern their behavior, not their thinking. Regardless of IQ level, children have to learn to recognize their feelings and to understand that good decisions can't be made when they are having "big" feelings.

Feelings are a function of needs. They are generated by needs, the most significant of which is the need to feel emotionally safe and important. Feelings are there to alert and protect us and to tell us how we are doing. *Even the most difficult, self-destructive or self-defeating behavior is generated by the need to protect ourselves at the emotional level.* Emotional safety is usually far more important to people than physical safety. This is especially true of wounded children. For this reason, it is essential to accept that feelings—whatever they are—are not good or bad. They are just there to do a job. What **is** good or bad is the way we **act** because

Even if you have identified children's strengths, it can still be challenging to teach them to use their strengths positively. This is particularly true of difficult children because they often do not think well. They act first, and may, or may not, think afterwards. They are usually unaware of what they are feeling and end up acting out their feelings rather than talking them out or thinking through a good course of action. The following method can help teach them to understand how their feelings and thinking work together to help them make good choices.

61

of our feelings. That is why it is important to learn how to let our actions be determined by how we think and not how we feel. This is a learned process that has to begin with the acceptance of all feelings and the recognition that good thinking can keep us from acting inappropriately because we are feeling upset.

Discuss this concept with the children in your care. Do it when everyone is feeling good and not in the middle of a major blow up or confrontation. Teaching these concepts will help children begin to realize that they **can** change how they act and react and will save you time in the long run. The goal is to help kids understand how feeling, thinking and acting are connected. Put these concepts into words that match the developmental level of the children you are working with.

Tell them:

- Everyone thinks and everyone feels.

- Feelings are only there to help us take care of ourselves.

- Some people have bigger feelings than others. (Using the descriptive word "big" to describe intense or strong feelings can help children and adolescents recognize that sometimes their feelings can seem overwhelming.)

- They probably have very big feelings.

- It is OK to have big feelings.

- It is **not** OK to hurt yourself or anybody else just because you have a big feeling,

- In order to make good decisions and be successful, it is necessary for your thinking parts and feeling parts to work together as a team.

- In order for your thinking (your brain) and your feelings (your emotions) to work together, it is important to pay attention to what you are feeling.

- It is also important to realize that you don't have to **do** what you **feel** like doing. You can **decide** (think) about what you want to do before you do something. This helps you stay out of trouble.

- Sometimes this takes practice.

- Things work out best when we keep things in their proper order – **Feel-Think-Act.**

- Trouble happens when we get things out of order and that usually means we **Feel-Act-Think.** This can cause us to do things that we really don't want to do.

  An example of this could be: A boy felt angry because his brother was constantly bothering him and he wanted him to stop. He was mad and so he hit his brother who started yelling for his mother immediately. Of course the boy got in trouble while nothing happened to his brother.

  If this boy had taken time to think when he first started to feel mad, maybe he could have figured out how to get his brother to stop bothering him without getting himself in trouble in the process.

  (Make up your own examples. There are usually plenty to choose from, but be careful not to use a child in your care as a bad example. After you discuss examples of how feelings lead to actions and acting without thinking first leads to trouble, then go on with the basics.)

- In order to avoid trouble like the above example, **talk to yourself as soon as you start feeling angry.** Once thinking begins, feelings will start to go away or get smaller. Then it is time to figure out what to do, how to act, or how to solve the problem at hand.

If this sounds simplistic or silly, be assured that it can be a very effective beginning for teaching children to understand the relationship between thinking, feeling and acting. Even the youngest children can be taught the differences and how to talk out, rather than act out a feeling, but someone has to take the time to teach them. ***They do not automatically know this.***

UNDERSTANDING YOUR OWN FEELINGS

CAUTION!
Remember:
When feelings
are intense,
thinking is
impaired.

Feelings/Impulse
+ Effective thinking
Appropriate action

Feelings/Impulse
+ No thinking
Inappropriate action

Teaching children and adolescents about the connection between feeling, thinking and acting is the first step in teaching them about choices. Teaching them about choices is the only way to avoid power struggles with these children and the best way to conserve your personal energy.

Children need to understand that inappropriate actions are usually caused by strong feelings. This is also true of the adults working with them. Since difficult children are often emotionally intense people, they have the ability to elicit equally intense reactions from the adults working with them. Many negative and challenging encounters with difficult children happen when either the child or the adult working with them are feeling extremely emotional. Usually the emotion is anger. (See GUIDELINES FOR WORKING WITH DIFFICULT KIDS).

Since emotions are functions of needs, it is important to remember that our own emotional responses to children are related to our own needs. Try to be aware of your own needs. For instance, some of us have an imperative need to be judged as competent and successful in our work. When children we are working with do things that impede our success, we can feel very threatened which in turn engenders anger in us. *Anger is a protective emotion.*

The first step in resolving an angry encounter with a child is to recognize that effective problem solving **cannot** take place until everyone's emotional intensity is diminished. The second step is to maintain or regain your own emotional equilibrium so that you can lead the child through a constructive thinking process. You, too, need to understand it is OK to have big feelings but **not** OK to act on what you feel. It is foolish to expect yourself not to have "big feelings" when you work with difficult kids.

In order to keep your own cool and get the child to make a good choice, remember the formula shown at the left. Teach it to the children you work with. Help them understand themselves and the importance of being able to engage their thinking processes before they act. Teach them to let their brain lead their actions instead of their feelings. This is the first stage of helping children understand the power of being able to make choices about their lives.

Remember to Keep it S-I-M-P-L-E

The S-I-M-P-L-E system will help you set up standards of appropriate and acceptable behavior by explaining to children: "These are choices, these are the consequences and these are the benefits or rewards of your choices." The system helps eliminate angry reactions and battles of the will by defining expectations in the form of choices the child makes rather than demands you make.

It is based on two simple principles. The first is the age-old adage "an ounce of prevention...." You can set up a S-I-M-P-L-E system to help prevent unnecessary conflicts and struggles. The second is there is no need to try to **make** children behave when they can be taught to **choose** cooperation and to recognize that there are consequences to all choices.

It takes time and energy initially to put the S-I-M-P-L-E skills and strategies to work but the pay-off is great in time saved in arguments, discipline problems and other energy-draining and frustrating encounters with kids.

A S-I-M-P-L-E Explanation:

S **is for STRUCTURE** which simply means making sure that everyone is aware of the rules or limits, what happens when everyone follows the rules, and what happens when they don't.

I **is for INSTRUCT** which ensures that the kids know exactly what you want them to **do** and not just what you **don't want them to do**.

M **is for MONITOR** which is another word for watching or paying close attention so that you can be certain to follow through with whatever you have said you would do.

P **is for PRAISE** which is all too often forgotten in working with difficult kids. It is one of the most powerful tools for influencing behavior.

L **is for LAUGH.** More can be accomplished playfully than forcefully any day of the week. This is especially true with the willful, stubborn or oppositional child.

E **is for EMPOWER** or encourage which simply means teaching children **how** to think not just **what** to think.

The S-I-M-P-L-E system provides the basis for teaching children **Self-Control, Cooperation** and **Courtesy.** It is helpful to understand each aspect of the system as thoroughly as possible because initiating it with the children in your care may be challenging or even awkward at first. It will be worth the effort! Let us look at each aspect of this system, while keeping in mind that things that are "simple" are not always "easy" to accomplish in the beginning.

REMEMBER TO KEEP IT S-I-M-P-L-E . . .

SET UP THE STRUCTURE

Setting up the structure means explaining exactly what you want and expect children to **do**, and not just what you **don't want them to do.** Clearly defined structure is important and necessary for difficult children and adolescents because it helps them learn how to make choices about their own behavior and take responsibility for their actions.

🍏 *Make certain all limits/boundaries/expectations are clearly defined.*

The more clearly you can outline the standards of acceptable behavior the better. This takes time and commitment on your part because you must decide what you will and will not tolerate **before** any negative behavior occurs, and you must stick with your standards each and every time that behavior occurs. It also gives children and adolescents a focal point for appropriate behavior.

Many difficult children know a great deal about inappropriate or oppositional behavior and very little about positive behaviors. Keep in mind that it is easier for most of us to try to **do** something than **not do** something. Think about the last time you tried to break a bad habit. Chances are, the more you thought of not being able to do what you wanted the more you wanted to do it. Still, we are always trying to get difficult kids to **stop** doing something. It is much more effective to keep telling them what we want them to do.

One time I was working on a daily basis with a group of boys ages five to twelve all of whom had been diagnosed with Attention Deficit Disorder. Most were hyperactive as well. Our goal was to teach them the skills they needed to help them with their attention deficit and hyperactive behavior. We began by setting the goal of helping them behave like gentlemen. All the boys liked the sound of this goal even though they weren't quite sure what it meant.

Working with us was a young physician whom the boys liked very much, and we used the doctor as a role model for a gentleman. Soon we had a list of behavior goals we called "What is a Gentleman?" Over and over for the next six weeks of working with the boys we referred to our list. This reinforced for them that our **expectation** was that they could and would behave appropriately and just exactly what that meant which was a great deal more effective than a list of rules or do's and don'ts posted somewhere in the room. *Communicating positive expectations to difficult children is extremely important if we want good results.*

In this way, proper behavior becomes a matter of choice. Essentially you tell them "These are the choices. These are the consequences and these are the rewards." They **choose** how they want to behave. What then happens to them is clearly a consequence of their choices and not your whims or moods.

The time you spend outlining your standards for positive behavior is time invested in your own energy supply because structure helps keep the focus of conflicts and confrontations on the choices the child has made instead of on you as disciplinarian, police officer or judge.

⚫ Outline the consequences before the limits are tested.

The key to teaching children to make positive choices is not only setting the standards for appropriate behavior, it is clearly defining the consequences and rewards of choices they make **before** they break rules or test the limits.

Difficult children always test the limits. They always want to know if you really mean what you say and whether you will do what you say you will do. To be effective with these children you MUST be reliable and dependable. You have to be counted on to follow through with whatever consequence has been determined appropriate for a given situation. *Therefore it is essential to determine consequences in advance.* Often this simple step is overlooked in working with difficult kids because so much energy goes into fighting and struggling with them or trying to figure out what to do once they have broken the rules.

This part of setting up structure is definitely the most time consuming for you, but it is also the most time saving in the long run because it eliminates those "What now?" times when rules are broken and limits

They always want to know if you really mean what you say and whether you will do what you say you will do.

SET UP THE STRUCTURE

breached. It eliminates the necessity of deciding what to do about negative behavior when you are angry or upset. It also ensures that you don't set up inappropriate consequences that you may regret when you find yourself not following through with what you have said you will do.

Setting consequences in advance of negative behavior applies to the general rules and guidelines for your work setting or home. It also includes specific negative behaviors you want to see changed which will be discussed in more detail in the next chapter. Most of all, this process enables children to make choices about their own behavior by deciding between consequences and rewards.

🍎 Make the consequences fit the behavior.

Logical consequences are the best. I always like to tie the consequence to the desired behavior whenever possible. For example, "If you are in on time, you'll be able to go out tomorrow night," "If you come in after 11 p.m., you'll be giving up your next evening out," or, "If your clothes get to the hamper, I'll wash them; if not, I won't."

It is a practical strategy to let the consequences reflect the amount of time and effort you have put into getting the cooperation you want. For instance: "Every minute it takes for you to do what you have been told to do, is that many minutes that will be subtracted from your free time, TV time, play time"—or whatever they want and enjoy.

It is also wise to tie consequences to privileges and to make certain children understand that the many things they enjoy or get are privileges and not rights. I call this the "No Tickee, No Washee Rule" which comes from the story of the Chinese laundry proprietor who refused to return laundry to any customer who couldn't produce the proper ticket. In this case it simply means that *if you don't do..., I won't do....*

I sometimes urge parents and caretakers to put up a "no tickee, no washee" sign to remind them of this rule. One time I did this with a friend who was a single parent trying to make certain that her children were able to do all those activities that are supposedly designed to build self-esteem in children but frequently wear parents out.

She and I were trying to visit with each other one day. We lived in different towns and rarely had an opportunity to get together. This particular day we had spent the whole afternoon driving all over town in horrendous traffic transporting her children from one activity to another.

We had picked them up from school and began our trek dropping one off, picking up the other at ball practice, the tutors, tennis lessons and so on. When we finally arrived at her home that evening she was angry and distraught that the children had not done any of the chores they were supposed to do before they left for school. She had left the house before they had that morning. She was so upset, she yelled and carried on with the children and eventually ended up in her bedroom crying out of sheer frustration. She felt helpless to get them to do the simple tasks they needed to do to keep the household running smoothly.

I suggested to her that she needed the "No tickee, no washee rule" and wrote the phrase on a sticky note and put it up on the mirror in her bathroom. I told her this was to remind her that the children needed to be taught that if they did not do what they were **supposed** to do, they would not be permitted to do the things they **wanted** to do. If they couldn't find time to accomplish their chores, she would not find time to transport them all over town to do the things they enjoyed.

Once the kids got this message loud and clear, she began to see good results. Here again it was more effective to spell out specific consequences and rewards rather than trying to get the children to be "supportive" of their single mother's efforts to make a good life for all of them.

I suggest that teachers use the same principle in outlining consequences with disruptive and difficult students. Sometimes the most dedicated teachers or childcare workers believe that children will and should behave because they recognize and value the sincere efforts on their behalf. Perhaps they should, but usually they are not developmentally advanced enough to do this, or haven't been trained to think about others first, so it best to help make their behavior choices clear up front.

Your distress is **not** an effective consequence. *Difficult children can tune out the most intensely negative responses.* Neither is your pleasure the most effective reward or benefit for positive behavior.

You can be creative in figuring out effective consequences, keeping in mind that what may be a consequence to one child could be a reward for another. For example, to say to a child, "If you do this..., you can sit next to me at lunch," may be a reward for one child and a punishment for another. The same is true of "time out" as consequence for negative behavior. The isolation of time out may be a punishment for some kids and a reward for others.

Difficult children can tune out the most intensely negative responses.

69

Set up the Structure

Difficult kids need to think of something positive as an external focal point to keep them on task and out of trouble.

This is one reason that *the old standby school punishment of In-School Suspension is having little effect on difficult kids.* For many young adolescents, In-School Suspension provides a place of safety and extremely tight structure which is less demanding than the regular classroom. Therefore, they **prefer** In-School Suspension and are governed accordingly.

It is also why it is so time consuming to set up the behavior guidelines you want with the proper consequences to match. You have to be sure that a consequence is not a reward and vice versa. It means that you are most likely to succeed at setting up an effective structure if you know the child or children in your care very well.

Decide the rewards or benefits.

While it can be troublesome to try and identify all consequences of negative behavior, what usually gives adults working with these children more difficulty is the rewards for appropriate behavior. Many people believe it is wrong or counterproductive to provide rewards for positive behavior.

Often I hear, especially from teachers of the "old school," that "Good behavior should be its own reward" or "Why should we reward children for doing the right thing?" I agree with the former but we must recognize that the goal of our work with difficult children is to get them to choose good behavior often enough for them to experience the intrinsic rewards of good behavior. As for why we should reward children for good behavior, the reason is a matter of focus.

Difficult children have poor internal behavior management skills. *Clearly defined rewards or benefits for good behavior provide a focal point for difficult children.* This works in much the same way that the training in natural childbirth includes teaching the women to focus on their breathing as well as some external object in the room. The external focus helps keep their focus off the pain of the contractions. It is always helpful to keep our attention **off** that which we are trying to avoid. Why constantly think of chocolate cake if you are trying to diet? Better to think of the clothes you want to be able to wear again or how good you will look and feel when you shed those extra pounds. It helps to focus on the reward you will be giving yourself for the lost weight instead of what you can't eat at the moment.

In the same way, difficult kids need to think of something positive as an external focal point to keep them on task and out of trouble. They need this to prompt their awareness of the choices they must make about their behavior. It is easier for them to make a good choice if they can focus on something they want. The focus draws their attention away from whatever satisfaction they get from difficult or oppositional behavior. *It helps provide a substitute for the internal behavior management skills they lack.*

In working with the boys with Attention Deficit Disorder, we used a token system. This made it possible to reward positive behavior immediately. It also gave the boys something to think about besides what they weren't supposed to do.

One of our goals was to extend their ability to sit and attend to a specific task. We set up the structure this way: using a simple kitchen timer, we explained that they needed to keep both feet and all four chair legs on the floor and stay focused on the lesson for two minutes. If they could do this, they could then spend five minutes playing computer games, an activity they loved. If their feet or the chair legs came off the floor or they had to be told to attend to the lesson, then the timer would go back to zero and the time it took for them to get to do the activity they enjoyed was extended. They were also rewarded with a token when they could make it through two minutes without having to put the timer back to zero.

The boys soon caught on, and while it took six weeks to accomplish, they could eventually sit properly and attend for thirty-minute intervals. They would even say, "Don't set the timer. Let's just get it (the group lesson) over with." (Always aim for small successes first. This will be discussed further in the next chapter.)

This is not intended to be a description of the details of using a token system for behavior modifications. This information is available in Russell A. Barkley's book *Defiant Children: A Clinician's Manual for Parent Training*. What I do want to emphasize here is the importance of providing a focal point in the form of a reward to help difficult kids think about what you want them do.

It works well with kids of all ages and sometimes it works best to let the kids decide what would be a reward that would help them stay on task. They sometimes know what motivates them best. You've always got veto power if their idea is outrageous or impractical. Sometimes their ideas are better than yours.

One mother was very concerned about having to leave her children with their grandmother for a week while she went to a job training

SET UP THE STRUCTURE

Children don't mean to be unsupportive of their parent's endeavors, although it certainly feels that way from time to time.

program. The children thought grandmother's was boring and mother thought their attitudes would lead to trouble. She also wanted them to promise to behave because the new job was a great opportunity for her and she wanted them to be supportive.

Children don't mean to be unsupportive of their parent's endeavors, although it certainly feels that way from time to time. They just don't think in those terms. Difficult kids have trouble thinking well period. It worked much better for this mother to tell the children exactly what she expected them to do at grandmother's house, what would happen if they were cooperative and what would happen if they weren't.

In this case, she was willing to take them for a short vacation on the beach if they behaved properly. They agreed that they'd like to go to the beach but their ideas for a reward for positive behavior were much simpler and less expensive. One child wanted money because he was saving for a new skateboard and the other wanted an inexpensive toy. The children did very well with grandmother making everyone, mother, children and grandmother happy.

🍎 Explain their choices.

After you have set up all the structure including the consequences and rewards for the behavior you desire, you then can turn over the business of getting them to behave properly to the children themselves. They decide what they will and won't do and what exactly will happen as a consequence of their choices. They need to recognize they are free to make good or bad choices.

Force is not necessary or practical when it comes to trying to get them to do what you want. They have a choice. You say to them, "You can do this.... or that.... It's your choice." *Be prepared for them to make some poor choices from time to time.* This is inevitable and necessary. It is even OK as long as they understand that they, not you, will be experiencing the consequences of their choices. Just be prepared to follow through with your part of the process.

🍎 Be consistent. Always follow through with consequences.

Your part is to follow through with the consequences and rewards you have outlined calmly and consistently. Staying calm is essential for this process to work well because if you are upset, angry or agitated, the focus of what has just happened will be on you and your emotional reaction and **not** on their behavior and choices. The focus needs to stay on their choices so that it will be very clear that whatever is happening is something that they set in motion themselves.

Being consistent is equally important. In fact, nothing is more important! Inconsistency in your responses to inappropriate behavior reinforces the very behavior you are trying to eliminate. To encourage yourself to follow through consistently with whatever consequences or incentives you have outlined for a child, it may help to keep in mind one of the basic concepts of classic behavior modification techniques.

As you may know, behavior modification techniques are designed to help change, eliminate or reinforce specific behaviors. One of the primary principles of behavior modification is the concept of positive reinforcement for desired behavior, which simply means giving rewards or recognition for good behavior. In this method, the interval at which the reward is given is as important as the reward itself.

If the goal is to keep a person doing something you want them to do, then the most powerful interval of reinforcement is called intermittent reinforcement. This means rewarding them when they are doing what you want them to do, but giving the rewards at unpredictable intervals. Intermittent rewards keep the people acting in the way you want them to act in hopes of getting the rewards they want the next time they do it. The important thing to remember is that people will keep trying to see if the next time they do something will be the time they get the reward.

This same principle works in reverse. If children know that they will receive a **negative** consequence for inappropriate behavior only at unpredictable intervals, like when you are in a certain mood or when you aren't too tired or busy, they will keep doing what they are doing (the difficult or unacceptable behavior) because they will be willing to gamble that the negative consequence won't occur this time. This is how inconsistent follow through will end up reinforcing the very behavior you are trying to eliminate. It is better not to tell a child that he or she will receive a negative consequence for unacceptable behavior than it is to say it, but not follow through with your promise, *immediately, every time, all the time.*

*Staying calm is essential for this process to work well because if you are upset, angry or agitated, the focus of what has just happened will be on you and your emotional reaction and **not** on their behavior and choices.*

INSTRUCT: LET THEM KNOW WHAT YOU WANT THEM TO DO.

Positive expectations often get positive results.

One way to avoid the pitfalls of inconsistent responses to children's behavior is to be very specific about what you want them to do, not just what you don't want them to do. Too often we fail to recognize that many difficult kids have little experience with positive behavior. That is why it is so important to tell them clearly and precisely what you want them to do.

🍎 State your expectations clearly and positively.

This is really a simple step to take, but it has a definite impact in at least two ways. The first is that it helps difficult kids understand clearly what you expect of them. The second is that it leaves them with the sense that your expectation is that they **will** choose the positive behavior you have described. Positive expectations often get positive results.

Unfortunately, we often give children the idea that we expect them to do the wrong thing. It isn't really complicated to change this habit. It just takes effort and practice. For example, a parent or houseparent might say, "I expect to find your dirty clothes in the hamper," versus "Don't leave your room a mess." The first not only sets up a positive expectation, it gives specific instructions. Their idea of a "mess" and yours may be very different.

The same principle applies in other settings besides home. This is the reason for our "What is a gentlemen?" list that we used with the young boys and the same reason we explained exactly how we wanted them to sit in their chairs to attend to group work. Saying things like "Sit still" or "Pay attention" was not enough. It was much more effective to tell them, "Keep both feet and all four chair legs on the floor" and "Keep your eyes on me." Not only is this more specific, it is more positive.

🍎 Keep the rules simple and positive.

The guidelines you set need to be positive whenever possible. Here again, this is not difficult; it just requires your attention and some practice. The more positive you are with difficult kids the better. This can be as simple as saying "Speak softly" instead of "Quit yelling," or "Everyone in our family talks in a respectful tone of voice" versus "Don't talk to your sister like that."

Even when the setting you are working in requires so many rules and regulations that they have to be written down in detail, the emphasis needs to be on the positive behavior you want and expect. If you have to list things like: no gum chewing, no mini skirts or no running in the halls, you can either describe the behavior you want before you list the no's or you can turn the no's into positive statements like: walking only in the halls, skirts must be knee length, or candy and gum are for after school only.

Some rules have to be stated firmly and emphatically as in "Violent behavior will not be tolerated," but that does not mean that you have to be forceful. Force is rarely necessary or advisable with difficult children as it will often stimulate more aggressive behavior.

🍎 Be firm and respectful. Never threaten in any way.

Describing appropriate behavior is especially important with children who have a tendency toward aggressive and hostile behavior. Tell them exactly what you expect, and let your tone of voice be firm but not hostile, shrill, mean or nasty. *You may want to yell but don't. Never talk down to a child.* Deepen your voice but speak respectfully. Be authoritative which says, "I'm in charge here and I know what I am doing" but **not** authoritarian which says, "I'm the only one who matters and no one's rights matter but mine."

Threatening words, tones and gestures, which many of us experienced as a normal part of our early training, will most often have a negative rebound effect on the difficult children of today. *It will prompt them to react with aggression and hostility.* (See INTERIOR LANDSCAPES AND GUIDELINES FOR WORKING WITH DIFFICULT KIDS.) These children need instruction in appropriate behavior and they need role models for positive behavior, conflict resolution and anger management. You are the model. You must show them how people work out differences or deal with angry feelings without being destructive to themselves or others. Many times you are their only opportunity to see these skills and traits in action.

The old-fashioned authoritarian way of our parents must give way to a firm and gentle authoritative manner that says everyone must do the right thing, and I am confident that we will all work together to meet that goal.

MONITOR: PAY ATTENTION.

Children need supervision. Adolescents especially need supervision. They must know that someone is monitoring them all the time and will notice and respond if they make inappropriate or negative choices.

🍎 *Make sure they have your full attention once the structure is set.*

Unfortunately, whether you are dealing with difficult children in a work setting or at home, more and more demands are made on your time and less and less time is spent actually working with the children. Yet, there is no substitute for your time and attention! Children must be watched carefully—not just because they are prone to be difficult, but because they need to know that you mean business and that you are going to be there to help them make good choices. The goal is to teach them to act appropriately when no one is watching, but to do that, they first need to know that one way or another they are being monitored. I have worked with many difficult kids who had been on their own entirely too much for their own good.

Let children, especially teenagers, know "I'm watching— not to catch you doing something wrong but to make certain you know that you have my support and that what you do is very important to me." Time and value go hand in hand, and it is difficult to convey the message that children are valued if you are not able to give them time and attention.

Letting them know you are watching can be as simple as making frequent eye contact when you are with them all day long. It is easy to get distracted especially when you have many children in your care, but a simple nod of the head, a positive hand gesture or a wink can let them know that you're paying attention. You can even do this while you are doing something else. Undivided attention just isn't always possible but frequent eye contact lets them know that you are paying attention.

🍎 Let them know you have confidence that they can and will make good choices.

Be careful that when you let them know that you are watching, it is with the attitude of expectations for positive behavior. At least affirm their ability to make good choices. It is important when you are setting

You want to communicate that you care, you are monitoring, and you have positive expectations, but for the moment, you are also attending to other business besides them. This is a necessary part of helping children to develop self-control.

up the structure with kids that you say , "You're a smart person. You can make good choices. I'm confident that you will." Or if they have a particularly poor track record, as many difficult kids do, you can say, "I hope you will make a good choice for yourself. Remember that your choices will impact your life more than they will mine." This way you keep the focus on the consequences of their choices and not on your reactions to their choices.

Be clear about your expectations for them when they must be left alone.

Unfortunately it has become acceptable, even standard practice to leave children alone and unsupervised. Sometimes this cannot be helped but it does complicate the process of setting up an effective behavior management system. Children left alone regularly, without supervision, are at much greater risk of difficult behavior, both when they are alone **and** when they are supervised. They tend to perceive themselves as autonomous and independent and therefore resent supervision when it is provided.

If you must leave older children or adolescents alone often, be very clear with them that they are not free to do whatever they please simply because you cannot be there. Check on them regularly. Also let them know who will respond if they have an emergency, or if you suspect that they are not making good choices while you are not there. Make certain that they know that you are still supervising them and that you expect them to make good choices even if you are not there watching them.

Clearly define when your time is your own and what is expected of them while you are not with them.

Even though you want to convey the message that you are watching and paying attention, you also want to let the children you work with know that there are times when your time is your own. You want to communicate that you care, you are monitoring, and you have positive expectations, but for the moment, you are also attending to other business besides them. This is a necessary part of helping children to develop self-control.

In my family, as very small children, our mother taught us self-control in many ways, but one of the most memorable was the way that she taught us to behave when she wasn't watching. We used to believe

MONITOR: Pay Attention

They need to know that you do not have to be actively interacting with them every minute in order to be monitoring them and that you expect them to have self-control when necessary.

that our mother had eyes in the back of her head, which had the excellent effect of making us reluctant to misbehave when we thought she wasn't paying attention. A big part of the reason we believed she had eyes in the back of her head was because she did watch us when we didn't think we were being watched, and she responded immediately to any misbehavior. We were always shocked to find out she had seen us do something wrong when we didn't think she was looking. This fairly frequent experience did, however, have the effect of helping us learn to manage our own behavior without direct, obvious supervision.

We were also told exactly how we were **expected** to behave when she wasn't watching us, and there were pretty severe consequences if our behavior didn't live up to her expectations. This was another way that our mother helped us learn self-control. One of the most vivid memories of my early childhood was a time when my mother had asked my younger brother, sister and me to play quietly while she was in a different part of the house talking to a relative about a serious matter. She told us that her discussion was very important, and that she expected us to stay out of her space, and not be disruptive, or come into the room where she was sitting with her guest.

She even promised to take us out to eat afterward if we did what we were told while she was busy. Back in those days, going out to eat was a very big treat because this was before fast food restaurants. Nevertheless, we got carried away with our playing, and not only made too much noise, but we foolishly interrupted our mother's discussion with her guest. She then left her guest long enough to tell us that not only would we **not** be going out to eat when she finished, but we would be punished besides. I don't remember the punishment, but I'll never forget the terrible disappointment of missing out on that very special treat. I think we all learned a couple of memorable lessons that day. The first was to always take my mother at her word, and the second was the importance of managing our own behavior when she was not there watching us.

Difficult children need to learn this lesson if they are to be successful in the world. You can teach them this just the way my mother taught us: first, by watching when they don't think you are watching; second, by explaining exactly how you expect them to behave when you are **not** watching; and last, but most important, by following through with swift and significant consequences when they do not cooperate.

You do not even have to physically leave the children in your care alone to teach this valuable lesson. Many teachers, houseparents and childcare workers are unable to leave the children they work with for even short periods of time throughout the day. This makes it more important than ever to teach them to respect your need for undisturbed time. *They need to know that you do not have to be actively interacting with them every minute in order to be monitoring them and that you expect them to have self-control.*

One third grade teacher, who was not able to leave the room throughout the day, felt very strongly that children needed to learn this lesson. She explained to her students exactly how she expected them to behave when she was busy attending to other matters. She also taught her class that when she placed a certain sign in plain view on the edge of her desk, they were to work independently and **not** disturb her. The sign simply read, "The Teacher Is Out."

Setting up the consequences and benefits for teaching this skill is not difficult. If you set up the structure so that the children also have time they can call their own, when they can do what they want, then it becomes a matter of making sure they don't get free time if you don't get free time. Another possibility for a logical consequence is to increase your direct supervision of these children. You can say, "Since you don't seem to be able to work on your own, I will make sure you get all the supervision you need." You can then increase your supervision until the next time you want some "do not disturb," time and then let them try again to behave appropriately without direct supervision.

Even very young children can be taught to leave mama or the teacher alone for short times. In fact, it is best to begin teaching them this skill when they are young because they will need to be able to behave properly without one-on-one supervision by the time they go to kindergarten.

Many adults working or living with difficult kids stay worn out and weary because they believe that they should not, or dare not, give themselves even a moment's break. This is not necessary or advisable because the ultimate goal of all work with children is to teach them the skills they need to be independent and successful. Being able to maintain appropriate behavior without constant and intense supervision is the beginning of both independence and success.

Being able to maintain appropriate behavior without constant and intense supervision is the beginning of independence and success.

79

MONITOR: Pay Attention

🍎 Be Fair, Firm and Consistent.

These are the simple keys to keeping it SIMPLE. The difficulty is, of course, that what is simple is not always easy. Remaining fair, firm and consistent in your response to unacceptable behavior is indeed challenging for several reasons. First, it isn't always easy to determine what is fair. Second, sometimes firmness becomes harshness or the equally ineffective opposite, wishy washy. And third, it is hard to be consistent when our moods, energy levels and levels of tolerance tend to fluctuate. We end up responding to a child's behavior based on what we feel at the moment instead of responding according to the structure and guidelines that have been outlined for the child. Difficult as it may be at times, these three cornerstones of positive and effective adult/child relationships are well worth your efforts to achieve.

So what is fairness, what exactly does it mean to be firm and why is consistency so hard?

Fairness:

Fairness is vitally important to creating an emotionally safe relationship with kids and emotionally safety is what all human beings need if they are going to let go of their defensive (and usually self-defeating) behavior. The trouble is that determining what is fair is not always easy. Here are few guidelines which may be helpful.

Fairness does not mean sameness.

It isn't even realistic to try to treat every child exactly the same. Different children have different personalities and needs, and fairness doesn't mean having to treat them all as though they don't.

Fairness means that everyone will be treated with equal respect (adults, children and adolescents alike), and everyone will be given an equal opportunity to succeed.

Giving everyone equal opportunity to succeed might mean permitting one child to do something other children are not permitted to do. This could mean allowing a child whom you know to be dealing with a severe trauma or grief to move around the classroom more freely while the other children must stay in their seats. Or it could mean letting a child sleep with a light on, or come in after curfew (when this is arranged in advance) while others are not allowed to do these things.

The decision to allow a special privilege which might appear unfair to others must be based on what a child or adolescent needs to achieve a significant goal.

One eight-year-old girl I worked with had enormous difficulty getting up and ready for school in the morning, so much so that the early morning struggles left the entire family exhausted before the day had even begun. After determining that her disruptive morning behavior was not an expression of some significant fear or anxiety related to going to school, we set out to help her do the two things which were giving her (and everyone else) the most difficulty.

The goal was to help her deal with her feelings when she first woke up and get herself moving and ready without mother's constant supervision.

As part of that structure, we agreed that she would receive a special reward when she was able to achieve this goal. Now her siblings were getting themselves up and ready every day with no problem and no reward. Still, they did not complain or resent the fact that their sister was being rewarded for what they did with no problem. On the contrary, they wanted the morning chaos to stop and were perfectly willing for their sister to get whatever help she needed to succeed in that endeavor. They cared about their sister but they also wanted their mother to be less frantic and their mornings to be more peaceful.

The structure we set up for this worked well, and before long the little girl was getting up and ready for school without any problem and without a daily reward. Even though the initial reward seemed "unfair" at first glance, it was fair in the sense that it gave the girl the opportunity to achieve an important goal for herself and her family, although the other children could accomplish this task without any help and assistance.

It is extremely rare for children to resent or complain when other children are given extra help if they are reassured that they, too, will be helped when they need it.

On the rare occasion when children say something like "That's not fair!" and the time is taken to give a reasonable explanation of why the extra help or privilege is being given, they no longer object providing they believe that they, too, will be given extra help when needed.

Ask yourself, "What goal for this child can be achieved by allowing this extra help or reward?"

Of course the whole notion of fairness falls apart if a child knows or

MONITOR: PAY ATTENTION

Any tone that communicates fear, anxiety or neediness, will have a negative impact on your ability to get the compliance and cooperation you want from children.

senses that some children are given preferential treatment just because they are liked better or someone feels sorry for them. It can be easy to spend more time and give more attention to children who are easier to like. Be careful of your motives in giving extra time and attention to a child.

Special privilege or rewards granted for any reason other than special assistance in the achievement of a legitimate goal will lead to resentment from other children and a sense of insecurity on the part of the child involved.

While they may not be aware of their feelings at a conscious level, children readily feel insecure with adults who act in unpredictable or unfair ways. Even a child who is the beneficiary of unfair treatment will feel insecure with the adults who act unfairly.

FIRMNESS:

Firmness in your communication style with children will also communicate safety. Expressing firmness is primarily a matter of tone of voice, which communicates two things: how you feel about the person or persons you are talking to and how you feel about yourself. If you feel self-confident and respect yourself, it will be apparent in your tone of voice and chances are you will come across respectfully to others. If you feel insecure or afraid that you are going to be criticized for what you are doing, or you need the child's approval or cooperation to feel good about yourself, that will also come across in your tone. Any tone that communicates fear, anxiety or neediness, will have a negative impact on your ability to get the compliance and cooperation you want from children.

Communicating firmness is especially important when giving directions or outlining choices regarding behavior. It is simply stating your message in a no-nonsense manner and in a voice that is not harsh but does communicate the message that you are the one in charge. Children need to hear confidence and self-assurance in your voice. Your self-confidence inspires them to feel confident and safe with you and encourages them to trust that you will indeed follow through with the consequences you have outlined.

Adults working with kids tend to err in their attempts to appear firm in one of three ways. They may state their directions and requests for kids in such a meek, pleading manner that the children don't take them seriously and therefore end up having to be told over and over before they comply. They may talk down to the child with a tone of voice that says, "I'm better than you and you better not forget it." Or they may simply yell. Any one of these styles of communication sends the message that you are not in control which leaves kids with anxious, insecure feelings and an unwritten invitation to act out.

The first style of communicating meekly with a pleading tone of voice will not encourage cooperation or compliance. When you speak as though you are **hoping** to get cooperation or compliance instead of **expecting** to get it, most likely you won't. Often adults who talk to children this way have a great need to be liked or loved by the children in their care. They are afraid that if they come across too strongly the children will feel unloved or discounted and therefore not respond to them in a positive, loving way. Letting your authority show in your voice doesn't mean you have to sound mean or threatening, or that you have to yell. It just means that you have to sound like you mean what you say and you are not inviting an argument or starting a discussion. It also means that you have to be willing to be disliked for the moment in order to establish a genuinely respectful relationship with a child.

I have heard many parents, teachers and childcare workers plead with children to cooperate. The pleading sound in an adult's voice only invites oppositional and argumentative behavior because it communicates that you aren't really in charge, the kids are, and they set about to prove you right.

Perhaps the most detrimental and least effective (especially with teenagers) communication style is the tone of voice that communicates that you consider yourself superior simply because you are the adult. *Nothing will trigger anger and even rage on the part of children and adolescents quicker and more surely than any form of condescension or tone of superiority.* This is problematic with today's children because teachers and many adults working with difficult kids are used to believing that they have the right to come across in a superior manner because they are the adults.

Unfortunately, adults who sound arrogant or superior often feel just the opposite deep down inside. They feel insecure enough that they need the power of their position to give them confidence that they can keep things (including people) in control. Without realizing it, they communicate their insecurity in their condescending tone.

It isn't necessary to act superior or talk down to a child in order to be firm or communicate that you are in charge and mean business. I strongly believe it is essential not to use a tone of voice with a difficult, disruptive child that you would not use with a difficult, disruptive adult.

The pleading sound in an adult's voice only invites oppositional and argumentative behavior because it communicates that you aren't really in charge, the kids are, and they set about to prove you right.

MONITOR: Pay Attention

Consistency means being dependable and requires a commitment to sticking to your guns and doing what you say you will do.

It's easy to yell at kids. It tends to make us feel like we have done something useful. It relieves us of the hard job of setting up proper structure and consistently following through with consequences. Many adults have been known to yell at a child from time to time but adults who make it a standard communication style often feel fearful of making a mistake or being criticized. ***Yelling actually becomes a substitute for the risk of taking a stand.***

Unfortunately, it takes no time at all for children to become immune to a yelling, and most of all, it communicates the message that you are not in control of yourself. When you are not in control of yourself, and you are supposed to be in charge, kids feel insecure.

I'll never forget knocking on the door of a neighbor's house years ago only to have her open the door in mid scream. She continued to scream some command or threat at her kids while I stood there feeling embarrassed for her. After all, most of us don't like others to hear us scream, even if we think it's really not so bad. So I said something about how bad it feels to lose your cool, hoping to minimize her embarrassment. "Feel bad!? Feel bad!?" she said. "I don't feel bad. If I didn't scream I'd go crazy." Clearly her yelling was aimed at making herself feel better in the moment and not in getting any genuine cooperation from her kids. While I can't say for certain that her way of keeping herself from going "crazy" made her children feel insecure, I was witness to the fact that it didn't have much positive impact on their behavior.

Sometimes we can't help feeling like yelling at a child but actually giving into that feeling may mean everyone loses. Yelling not only will make kids feel insecure and cause them to act out more, but also will make you feel bad about yourself. You can be firm without yelling.

Consistency:

Consistency means being dependable and requires a commitment to sticking to your guns and doing what you say you will do. It means not letting kids do something one time and not another, or reacting with extreme consequences to a behavior one day and letting it go with a mere scolding the next time. Consistency creates emotional safety for children, and kids need to feel safe before they will let go of their defensive, negative behaviors. As important as it is, the question becomes, why is consistency so difficult to achieve and what can be done to make it easier to stay consistent in our responses to difficult and oppositional behavior?

There are three main obstacles to following through consistently with exactly what you have said you will do. The first two are, of course, stress and fatigue. When we get tired, we give in or we ignore behavior that we would address if we weren't so tired. The third is not setting up enough structure in the first place. Structure is making sure that everyone knows what is expected and what the rewards and consequences of actions will be...before they happen. If the rewards and consequences have already been decided then we don't have to try to decide what to do when a problem arises and we are too tired to think or make an effective response.

Staying consistent with your responses is so important that it makes sense for you to make taking care of yourself, by getting enough rest and recreation, a priority. Usually, taking care of yourself ends up at the bottom of the priority list. Perhaps if it could be seen as a necessary strategy for working with difficult kids, it could be moved up on the priority list. There just is no substitute for rest and recreation which are essential to dealing effectively with any kind of stressors.

Another important strategy for taking care of yourself is to keep the circles of control in mind and to stay focused on what you can and cannot control. Then give yourself credit and acknowledgment for your hard work even if you'd like to be acknowledged by someone else. You can give yourself what you want others to give you. It may feel silly or awkward at first but it does work. After a while you'll even begin to realize that your good opinion of yourself is the most important opinion of all and feels as good as a pat on the back coming from someone else. We all need acknowledgment, encouragement and praise, which leads us to the power of praise, the next facet of the S-I-M-P-L-E method.

PRAISE: COMMENDATION COUNTS.

Difficult children rarely get praised. You may even find yourself saying "So what's to praise? I'll praise them when they start doing what is expected of them." These words express an understandable feeling but not an effective strategy for working with difficult kids. Praise is one of the most practical and powerful behavior management strategies. It is also the most overlooked or misused. Be careful and generous with your praise. It can inspire surprising results.

PRAISE: COMMENDATION COUNTS.

The following guidelines will help you praise the difficult children in your care and enjoy the benefits of this excellent communication and management skill.

Remember how praise affects you.

Take just a moment to close your eyes and recall the last time you received a sincere compliment or word of acknowledgment. Now recall how you felt at the time, and then recall how you felt afterward. Last, think about how those feelings affected your actions or performance.

Chances are your memories were quite pleasant. You recalled not only feeling good, but you also remember feeling more motivated to do your best. No doubt about it, praise is a great motivator. We all enjoy being commended for our efforts and achievements. It makes us feel proud and inspired to do even better. Everyone knows that from personal experience, it's not just a theory or a good idea. We all **know** it.

Praise doesn't cost anything. It doesn't require training or special expertise. Praise is simple, easy, and makes people feel good about themselves, work harder and do better. It even feels good to **give** praise. The question, then, is why is it so rare? Why don't employers, parents, teachers and childcare workers (all of whom are invested in getting people to perform better) do it more often?

Understand your reluctance to praise.

So many people are reluctant to praise, even knowing the positive effects it can elicit for three common reasons. The first is the belief that praise should be given for perfect performance only because anything else will inhibit striving. It is what I hear most often from parents of difficult but high achieving kids. It goes something like this, "Sure, she got a good score on her SAT, but she could have done better and she should have worked harder," or "Okay, I admit he didn't have one angry outburst this week, but what about his room? It's still a disaster."

From this viewpoint, all achievements are measured against possible perfection, and anything short of perfection isn't worthy of praise. We are a society of success and results-oriented people. We measure and assess progress but only reward results, and praise becomes a valued reward given only for total achievement.

This reason is also heard often in the case of difficult kids. The typical comment is "So what's to praise? Just look at all her behavior." These kids cause so many problems for themselves and others that it can be hard to find something to praise, especially if overall perfection or even total goal achievement is the standard of measure.

The second reason for a reluctance to praise is the belief that praise will be taken as blanket approval. It's as though it is best not to acknowledge anything good children do lest they think the praise means approval of their not-so-good behavior. The fear is that any kind of praise might give them the idea that we think they are okay the way they are. This leaves difficult kids with serious praise deprivation since they usually have great need for improvement in many areas.

The final reason that praise is often withheld is because some adults feel over-responsible for a child's behavior and achievements. Whether they are parents, teachers, or are responsible for a child in some other capacity, they are unable to recognize the autonomy of the child and therefore feel that the child's behavior is a reflection on them by which they too will be judged. If children are difficult, parents have a tendency to feel embarrassed or even ashamed and are in constant fear of criticism from other adults. This fear and their sense of identifying their personal worth with the negative behavior of the child leaves them unable to praise even a significant achievement.

All three of these common obstacles to praise inhibit the use of a very powerful and effective behavior management strategy. Praise will not keep a child from trying harder. In fact, the reverse is true. It will not cause them to believe that all their behavior is okay simply because some positive action or achievement is acknowledged. Difficult children are acutely aware of adult disapproval even when they seem impervious to it. Praise will not be mistaken for blanket approval. Neither will it invite criticism from others because the children for whom you are responsible are less than perfect. Even if you have some responsibility for the actions of the children in your care, they are ultimately responsible for their behaviors and are not expressions of your self-worth. It's okay to acknowledge their positive strengths.

Not only is praise not harmful in any way, it will foster self-esteem, confidence and positive behavior. It will make the child feel good. It will make you feel good. It is the great encourager and is essential to working effectively with difficult kids.

Difficult children are acutely aware of adult disapproval even when they seem impervious to it. Praise will not be mistaken for blanket approval.

PRAISE: COMMENDATION COUNTS.

Steps along the way have to be recognized. This means acknowledging efforts as well as small successes.

🍎 Praise the deed not the person.

Praise should always focus on behavior or actions, not on personality or personhood. Say, "You did great." Do not say, "You are a great guy." Say, "It was so good to hear you use words to express your anger instead of hitting or yelling." Do not say, "You are so good because you are learning to say your feelings."

Difficult kids don't feel very good about themselves, even those who act quite arrogantly. Complimenting their personhood just makes them feel uncomfortable. They will discount instead of enjoy and take in your praise because they think, "If you really knew me, you wouldn't say that." Praising the act frees them up to enjoy their own achievements even when they haven't yet developed a true sense of self-esteem.

🍎 Praise the process not just total success or achievement

It is important to praise along the way to a goal. A "great going" can go a long way to keep a child striving toward a goal. Praise should be part of the process of striving, not just a reward for achievement.

One of the reasons school tends to be such a distressing and negative experience for some children is because, in most school settings, there is little if any recognition for effort. Achievement is all that matters. Kids who have difficulty succeeding at the pace of their peers get left out of any positive feedback. Sometimes their acting out is an expression of the frustration they feel because no matter how hard they try, all that matters is the academic grade. How hard they try counts for nothing.

Steps along the way matter very much. Just ask anyone who has built a house. It's not just getting the house completed that counts. It's how well each part of the construction process is done that matters, especially when it comes to actually living in the house.

This same principle applies to all work with difficult kids. It's not just the final outcome that matters. Steps along the way have to be recognized. This means acknowledging efforts as well as small successes. Whatever the long term goal for a child is, make sure that the small steps along the way are recognized. If, for instance, the goal is to get a child to quit disrupting the class everyday, then set the goal of getting the disruptive behavior stopped for an hour, or even a half-hour, or whatever short time is most likely achievable. Set the child up to succeed! Then praise the efforts the child makes, not just the success. Tell the child, "I noticed how hard you tried to stay quiet this morning. I'll bet you make it next time."

🍎 Grades and other rewards for achievement are not substitutes for praise.

Years ago my husband was teaching 8th grade science in a rural middle school. One evening while he was grading papers, he showed me a fill-in-the-blank test that one student had turned in, and asked me what I thought of it. The student had scribbled, just like a small child does before he or she knows how to write, in every blank on the page. I asked him what was the boy trying to achieve, thinking maybe the boy had just been acting out. My husband explained that the boy could not read or write, and had been passed on to eighth grade because of his age. My husband had established a positive relationship with the boy and the boy knew he liked him. This was the first time the boy had not turned in a totally blank test. The scribbles were his effort to let my husband know that he was trying. And he was. He was doing his best. My husband made the decision that the student needed and deserved to be acknowledged for his effort.

Among the many sad things about this story is that, for whatever reason this boy had not learned to read or write, his low levels of academic achievement meant he rarely experienced any kind of positive feedback in school. If all acknowledgment and encouragement come from academic achievement only, then some kids miss out entirely.

Many children and adolescents are missing out. More and more children who do not, or cannot, achieve success academically are being placed in regular classes with students who achieve at normal rates. Failure becomes a regular part of their daily life experience. Grades, which are meant to be a measurement of academic achievement only, become the measurement of the child's entire personhood and worth, and the only chance a child has to be positively recognized.

Never to be acknowledged, encouraged or commended for anything is indeed deprivation. It starves the spirit and leaves children pained and emotionally wounded. Emotional pain is one of the most significant reasons children act out. Healthy, frequent praise and acknowledgment for sincere effort or simple successes can help children believe in their own worth.

I am not suggesting that academic performance is not important, or that children shouldn't be graded for it. I am suggesting that it should not be used as the sum total of a child's value or potential.

Never to be acknowledged, encouraged or commended for anything is indeed deprivation. It starves the spirit and leaves children pained and emotionally wounded.

🍎 Expressions of affection are not substitutes for praise.

Just as a grading system is not meant to be a substitute for praise and sincere commendation, neither do words and gestures of love and affection substitute for praise. Many parents believe that telling their children they are loved has the same impact as acknowledging their efforts and achievements. Children need to know they are loved, but they also need to know that they are appreciated and that their parents recognize their efforts and talents.

This also is true of teachers and other professionals working with children. Expressions of love and affection are important, but they are not the same as recognizing a simple achievement or a special ability.

One of the teachers I remember most from my own high school years was an American government teacher who insisted that I enter an essay contest sponsored by the local Civitan Club. He told me that he thought that I could win and was therefore making the essay a required assignment for me, but not the rest of the class. I won second place in that contest, but more importantly, I have never forgotten his belief in my talents, especially since they were talents I was completely unaware of myself.

🍎 Praise unexpectedly.

Nothing feels as good as receiving a word of praise when you're least expecting it. Watch the kids in your care carefully and give a "great going" or even a positive gesture like a thumbs up when you see them do something positive. Even a simple, "All right!" can work wonders, especially when it comes to unexpected acknowledgment.

🍎 Praise the littlest act.

Praise can be so simple and doesn't have to be reserved for some grand accomplishment. The problem, of course, with difficult kids is that we become so accustomed to dealing with unacceptable behavior that we forget to notice the positive things these kids do.

One day when I was working with a group of boys with Attention Deficit Disorder, I was instructing the boys about making signs we were going to put up around the room. I said to one little eight year old, "You make a sign that says 'No Kid Zone'," to which he promptly replied, "Now, Ms. Joyce you know I can't read." Of course, his reading problems had been discussed in the past, but I hadn't thought of that when I told him to make the sign, and I didn't think it needed to be a reason for him to feel inept about the simple task of making a sign. I said, "You go over there and make a sign with the same letters in the same order as Jim (one of the other boys) and you'll have your sign." He did just that and brought me his sign when he finished.

I said, "That's a good looking sign. I'm impressed." Not making anything of his original belief that he couldn't do it, I said, "Let's go put it up," which we did. After it was posted on the door to the staff room, I said, "Now, tell me what it says." He looked at the sign and answered, "It says No Kid Zone." I said, "Look at you—you're reading. And you told me you couldn't read. Now I don't know what to think." He just grinned and we went on about our business.

Two days later I was doing a reading group with the boys, and not wanting to embarrass this young man, I just skipped over him when it came his turn to read. Immediately, he said, "Now Ms. Joyce, you know I can read." I said, "Well go right ahead and when you want us to tell you a word, you just look up, otherwise we'll wait for you to sound it out." He then proceeded to read aloud about every other word.

Even the simplest praise, for the smallest thing, can have great power. Commendation does count.

Even the simplest praise, for the smallest thing, can have great power. Commendation does count.

REMEMBER TO KEEP IT s-i-m-p-L-e

LAUGH AND BE PLAYFUL.

It is easy when working or living with difficult kids to get so caught up in the struggle that all the fun goes out of being with these children. This is especially sad since sharing in their natural playfulness and creativity can be one of the greatest joys of working with these kids. Playfulness is also one of the best strategies for changing difficult behavior.

When you are using humor and playfulness with difficult kids it can help to the keep the following suggestions in mind:

🍎 Humor builds trust.

Since playfulness and laughter are part of their natural way of being in the world, children are inclined to trust people who can get into their world with laughter and play. Trust is the cornerstone of positive relation-

LAUGH AND BE PLAYFUL.

ships, and when trust increases, difficult behavior is much more amenable to change, especially since most negative behavior is a defense against past hurts and disappointments.

Humor can get the results you want with a child when all else fails. Even though there are times when it is important and necessary to communicate in a no-nonsense manner, it can be equally effective, at other times, to be playful. Don't be afraid to let yourself have fun, joke around a bit, and be playful, even when you are telling kids things that are quite serious. If you set up a clearly defined structure and establish a good working relationship with children, they will know that you mean for them to behave and cooperate even when you are having fun with them.

Gentle and loving teasing can often replace nagging.

Healthy teasing can help children develop a good sense of humor and teach them not to take themselves too seriously. It can also help them develop a different view of their own behavior.

One time a thirteen-year-old girl, living in a group home, was driving both staff and fellow residents crazy with her habit of whining. She whined everything she had to say to everyone. Everyone begged her to stop.

Structure was set up to make her aware of her whining ways and to encourage her to speak in a normal tone of voice. This did not work. The other residents were encouraged to tell her frankly, but politely, how her whining affected them. That didn't work. The staff spent considerable time in weekly staff meetings coming up with strategies to change this behavior. Nothing worked!

Finally, one day when she came up to me and asked me something in her very best whine, I responded in an equally obnoxious whine. She stopped in her tracks and looked at me. She said something else and I whined back. I kept an absolutely straight face even after she started to giggle. This went on for a while and before long she quit whining.

Everyone had tried to change this behavior to no avail. Lots of time and attention had gone into the problem. Then in one relatively short incident of playful teasing, the difficult behavior was permanently changed.

Never let teasing or playfulness embarrass a child.

Part of the reason the playful exchange between this girl and me worked is because we already had a positive relationship and *she trusted that I was playing with her and not making fun of her.* She knew me well enough to know that I would not intentionally embarrass her for any reason.

Teasing a child is a delicate matter. It must be done with the utmost respect for the child's sensitivities and never in a way that truly embarrasses one child in front of another. Most troubled and difficult children carry around a deep and unconscious sense of shame and humiliation. Embarrassment can trigger shameful feelings and subsequently provoke negative behavior.

Be willing to let them take the lead in play.

Mutual respect is the most important concept you have to model for children and it applies to this issue as well. Let the kids you work with know that you can enjoy their humor and sense of fun and not just the other way around.

One time the adolescent girls I was working with decided to have "tacky day," and they wanted me to participate, which meant that I had to come to work wearing something outrageous and tacky. I said I would. That morning I had to attend a board meeting with our benefactors in the downtown area. I did wear my normal business attire for that meeting which included a lunch at a downtown restaurant. After lunch though, I went into the restroom and put on my "tacky" outfit and then tried to make it out of the restaurant without being seen. I'm still not sure if I accomplished that goal, but I was able to arrive on the campus of the girl's residence wearing my tacky clothes which, silly as it made me feel, sure impressed the girls. We went on to have a "tacky fashion show" which was one of the most creative fun times I ever had with kids.

The best part of being playful with kids and letting them "play" with you is not that it helps change negative behavior— the best part is that you have fun, too!

REMEMBER TO KEEP IT S-I-M-P-L-**E**

EMPOWER: TEACH THEM *HOW* TO THINK, NOT JUST *WHAT* TO THINK.

Children must learn that they can control their own behavior and that it is their responsibility to do so, not yours or anyone else's. This is

EMPOWER: TEACH THEM *How* TO THINK, NOT JUST *WHAT* TO THINK.

The goal of all work with children is to help them learn how to feel powerful, competent and emotionally safe, without hurting themselves or others in the process.

the essence of empowerment. To empower children is to teach them **how** to think, not just **what** to think. They have to learn to think about what they do and about the choices they make about their own behavior. They have to recognize that their behavior is a matter of choice, and it is their job, and in their best interests, to make good choices for themselves. It is not your job to **make** them behave. Your job is to teach them how to make good choices about their own behavior, and you do this by defining their choices, and the consequences and benefits of those choices and then, of course, following through consistently.

🍎 Teach them to understand their choices.

A great deal of unacceptable behavior is an expression of children or adolescents need to feel powerful which makes them feel, at least temporarily, like they are emotionally safe and in control. The goal of all work with children is to help them learn how to feel powerful, competent and emotionally safe, without hurting themselves or others in the process.

In the process of setting up clearly defined structure you help children understand their choices. If you let kids make choices instead of trying to make them behave, they will develop a sense of their own power which is simply their ability to feel competent and take care of themselves.

🍎 Freedom to think and disagree is not the same as freedom to do whatever they choose.

There is no need to be afraid that if you give children freedom to think for themselves and make their own choices, they will not do what you want. The reverse is true. When you tell them what they have to do, they may feel a need to prove that they don't. When you give them choices and help them understand the consequences of those choices, they are more apt to feel the freedom to act in their own best interests.

They also need the freedom to disagree with you. Freedom to disagree is not freedom to do whatever they choose, but it is an essential element of empowerment. Children need to have their opinions and choices validated even when they don't agree with you. This means respecting their right to have opinions, and is not the same as agreeing or approving of their opinions or ideas.

Giving children freedom to disagree and express opinions of their own is easier if you don't take their opposition to your ideas and suggestions personally. Their opposition is not about you. It is about their need to prove something to themselves. Keep in mind that their need for independence is healthy and requires them to push up against authority. They aren't always just trying to discount you and your authority, even though it may seem like that quite frequently.

It isn't necessary for disagreements to be expressed disrespectfully by you or them, but it is necessary for children to be allowed, and even taught, how to disagree properly, if they are to be empowered to make good choices.

Of course, sometimes, with adolescents especially, it is necessary to keep them from making choices that are permanently damaging or even deadly. But the sooner they begin to learn how to make good choices, the less prone they will be to make the more dangerous choices when they begin to establish their independence.

Sometimes parents, and even those of us who work with children, forget that our mission is to teach children to be independent of us. We must teach them self-control and proper behavior, but we must ultimately help them learn to rely on their own inner strength and not on us, or our approval. If all controls on children's behavior are external, they will never learn to develop inner strength or self-control. Teaching self-control requires external control at first, but can only be fully realized when children learn that they can make good choices and recover from bad ones.

🍎 Let them learn from their mistakes.

Children will learn from their poor choices as well their good ones. Let them live with the consequences of their choices. Don't rescue them. Rescuing sends the subtle message that you believe they can't do it on their own. Letting them live with the consequences of their choices is the only way to effectively teach them the connection between choice and consequence.

Once a poor choice has been made you can help a child review what happened and why. *This does not mean criticize or condemn. No good comes from criticism.* It only serves to make people feel bad, which is not the same as helping them take a clear look at what they need to do differently next time. Encourage them to think about what they are doing or have done instead.

Say to them, "Let's think it through. What could you have done differently?" It is amazing how seldom children are asked this question. Encourage them to figure things out for themselves. It's true that sometimes they will come up blank and say their old standby, "I don't know"

Say to them, "Let's think it through. What could you have done differently?" It is amazing how seldom children are asked this question.

EMPOWER: TEACH THEM *HOW* TO THINK, NOT JUST *WHAT* TO THINK.

or something that sounds like that. Then you just "walk them through the thinking process" starting with, "Well, this choice didn't work out for you so there must be some other way to handle the situation. What could it be?" You may even have to say, "I wonder if the next time you might try...." Sometimes they really can't think of what might work for them. This is still more instructional than saying, "You should have known better," or "You should have done this or that." Your goal is to get them to recognize the concept of actions beget consequences.

🍎 Encourage them when they make mistakes.

Everyone needs encouragement and most of us need a lot more of it than we get. Never is this need greater than when we have just made a big mistake. Even when kids are super defensive and trying not to take responsibility for their mistakes, it can help them if you can affirm that they'll probably choose differently next time. You can say, "Oh well, even if it's true that this 'wasn't your fault,' I'm guessing you won't do it again because you're a smart person."

There are lots of ways to encourage. The best way is the simplest. Sometimes when we set out to encourage a child we end up lecturing. Then they feel like we are only pointing out their failures instead of encouraging them to believe in their strengths.

Often, instead of offering encouragement we are quick to point out what went wrong and why. We say, "See, that's what you get for not studying enough." We are problem solvers and we want them to be. It's good to teach them how to problem solve and to be able to figure out what happened and why, but encourage them first.

Think of the word encourage. It means to give courage. Most often this means a simple "You can do it." Encouragement is a highly effective substitute for criticism. Remember, it's hard to be a kid. There's so much to learn and so many standards to measure up to, and the whole process can be overwhelming and mighty discouraging. Encouragement keeps your focus, and theirs, on what is possible, and focusing on positive possibilities enhances the opportunity for success. Yours and theirs.

🍎 Beware of letting comfort and encouragement substitute for structure.

While some adults are prone to over-criticize children, others are prone to let their encouragement and understanding become a substitute for letting children face the consequences of their own choices. Often, these are adults who were treated harshly as children themselves and they project their own need for comfort and encouragement onto the children in their care. They mean well because they don't want children to feel hurt or humiliated by their mistakes. They don't always understand that when you take away opportunities to experience the consequences of mistakes, you rob children of their personal power, especially the power of resilience.

One of the most important things we have to teach kids is how to face and overcome disappointments. To be successful, we have to know how to encourage and comfort ourselves when we fail. Every great champion athlete has lost a competition somewhere along the way to the championship. Without the ability to sustain discouragement and disappointment, a person cannot achieve success.

🍎 Teach them to encourage themselves.

Children have to learn how to fall down, pick themselves up, brush themselves off, and try again if they are going to be able to achieve any significant goal. Even the great homerun king Babe Ruth struck out far more often than he hit home runs. Teach kids the basics of resilience.

Difficult kids, by nature, are impatient with themselves. They do not know how to encourage or comfort themselves. They have strong tendencies to beat themselves up, or to project their anger with themselves onto the people around them, thus creating chaos. Talk to them about how they talk to themselves, and teach them the art of positive self-talk. Help them learn how to say kind things to themselves.

The way to teach this behavior is to model it in two significant ways. First, you have to be able to encourage yourself when you falter or make mistakes, especially when you make mistakes in your interactions with the kids in your care. Your own self-talk needs to be positive and encouraging. It is okay to admit to yourself that you might not have handled a situation very well, but you will do better next time. If you can be kind to yourself, and say comforting things to yourself, then you can teach kids to encourage themselves.

The second way to model encouragement is to say comforting things to them. Often adults are so focused on getting kids to act properly, be cooperative, and achieve, that they forget that children have a great deal to learn on the way to adulthood and independence, and at times, the process is very dis-

Children have to learn how to fall down, pick themselves up, brush themselves off, and try again if they are going to be able to achieve any significant goal.

EMPOWER: TEACH THEM *HOW* TO THINK, NOT JUST *WHAT* TO THINK.

couraging. When children goof up, fumble, fail, or make bad choices, teach them how to encourage themselves by saying encouraging things to them.

It is tempting to criticize instead of encourage. "I'm sorry this happened; you'll be okay," or "You did your best; you'll get it next time" are all ways to comfort and encourage. Saying "It's okay to make a mistake" teaches children to be kind to themselves and keep on trying. Children (and adults) who are kind to themselves are also kind to others.

Your personal energy supply will be greatly affected by how you encourage yourself and the children in your care. When children feel empowered to make choices about their behavior, and overcome their mistakes, it does not require such large supplies of your personal energy to get them to do, or make them do, the right thing.

WORKING THE HARVEST

- CHOOSING THE B-E-S-T STRATEGY

- CAN YOU IDENTIFY THE CHILD'S STRENGTHS?

- INTERVENTION STRATEGIES

- INEFFECTIVE STRATEGIES (STRATEGIES THAT WILL BACKFIRE)

- CRISIS INTERVENTION IN THE CLASSROOM

- TIPS FOR TEACHERS: PLANNING A PARENT-TEACHER CONFERENCE

- HOW TO HELP A CHILD BE A SUCCESSFUL STUDENT

- GUIDELINES FOR WORKING WITH CHILDREN OR ADOLESCENTS WITH
  ATTENTION DEFICIT DISORDER

- BURNOUT PREVENTION STRATEGIES

- A FINAL WORD ON HOPE...

CHOOSING THE B-E-S-T STRATEGY

Some strategies are effective with some children in some situations but not others. Choose your strategy carefully and only after you have taken time to assess the situation thoroughly.

When a child does not respond in the way you expected or hoped, take the time to consider as many factors as possible which might be contributing to or causing the difficult behavior **before** you decide what to do next.

To avoid ineffective, energy-draining reactions, plan your intervention strategy in advance by taking time to make as comprehensive of an assessment of the child's behavior as time will permit. "What is BEST for this child" will help direct the assessment process. Remember, time **spent** in planning effective strategies will result in time **saved** in conflict management and power struggles.

Remember: Your goal is to respond effectively, NOT react.

A carefully chosen **response** can prevent an automatic **reaction** which has proven ineffective in the past. **Use the following guidelines based on the acronym B-E-S-T to judge which strategy is likely to be most effective.**

BEHAVIOR: Observe Everyone's Behavior Carefully.

What is the child doing?

What are you doing?

What is the class doing?

What do you want the child to do instead?

What positive quality/strength may be hidden in the negative
    behavior? (see CAN YOU IDENTIFY THE STRENGTHS?)

CAUTION: *Know the goal of your intervention.*

EVALUATE: Look Carefully At Underlying Issues.

What do you think the child is feeling?

BEWARE: *Your assumptions may be wrong.*

What need is the child attempting to meet?

What need are you attempting to meet?

How does the class respond to this behavior?

What time of the day does it usually occur?

What strategy have you already tried?

What do you imagine happening to this child if he or she is not able to change this behavior?

Is the behavior constant or intermittent?

Does this child act this way with other teachers? All the time?

Do you or any of your colleagues ever do the same thing to the child?

How does the child respond when you ask, "What could you have done differently?"

What does the child say about his or her behavior?

STRATEGY: *Choose a strategy with your goal in mind.*

Does the strategy meet a need? Yours? Theirs?

Does it teach?

Could you utilize others in your strategy?

Have you already tried it?

Did you get the results you wanted?

Is it clear, direct and specific about what you **want**, not what you **do not** want?

Is there a payoff/reward for the child?

Does it include **choice**?

Does it address the child's behavior and not the child's character?

Will it teach by experience, by consequence, by instruction?

TEACHING TOOL: *What and how will your strategy teach?*

BEWARE: If it requires instruction, have you been *clear, concise and concrete?*

Will it impact the child in the here and now?

Does it include a prevention plan?

CAUTION: *With difficult children, a lecture is usually an ineffective teaching tool.*

Modeling is an important teaching tool but not enough.

Remember: Some things are best taught by repetition.

Be willing to repeat yourself over and over.

CAN YOU IDENTIFY THE CHILD'S STRENGTHS?

LOOK FOR AND FOCUS ON HIDDEN PERSONALITY STRENGTHS

Focusing on a child's underlying strengths makes it possible to re-direct negative behavior into healthy channels. It also helps foster self-esteem, and create future for these children. As much as possible, try to distinguish between the true character of a child and the child's difficult behavior. Even the most troublesome children or adolescents have character strengths that underlie their difficult behavior. It isn't always easy to discern the positive strengths of difficult children; however, once strengths are identified, it is possible to redirect the unacceptable behavior to more positive channels. Redirecting this behavior will not only minimize the problematic behavior, but it will save time and your personal energy as well.

Uncovering character strengths requires creativity and effort. Consider the following possibilities:

🍎 Defiant behavior can hide leadership potential

When defiance comes easy, you are usually dealing with a potential leader; after all, this nation was founded by a small group of defiant landowners who decided to stand down the most powerful nation on earth, and won. Defiant people challenge authority. They are not easily led. The ability to defy authority can be a useful trait when channeled in a healthy direction.

REDIRECTED DEFIANCE:

Help the child understand his or her leadership potential. Structure opportunities for the child to be placed in leadership roles even small chances to lead, like leading a line of children to lunch can help. Make leadership opportunities contingent on compliant behavior.

With older children or adolescents, make them do writing and thinking exercises which distinguish between defiance of law and order, and defiance of injustice, discrimination and inequality. Help them discover (research and report) how important healthy defiance is to society, and how healthy defiance is expressed. Make them write letters to Congressional leaders, editors and other power sources. Be creative.

🍎 Attention-seeking behavior can hide persistence and perseverance

Attention-seeking behavior often requires persistence and perseverance. Both of these traits are admirable and necessary for long term success in almost any endeavor. These people do not give up even in the face of personal rejection. They also have many leadership qualities and tend to be happiest in relationships with others.

REDIRECTED ATTENTION SEEKING:

Acknowledge the positive aspects of this behavior. Give these children a chance to get some one-on-one attention. Make one-on-one time contingent on cooperation and appropriate group behavior. Teach them how to use their persistence and perseverance to get a really hard job done. Set up projects for that purpose. Let them lead the group in a task that requires these traits.

Clowning/show-off behavior can hide creative thinking and talent

Clowning, joking and showing off serves to help avoid the nitty gritty work of required tasks, but it can also make required tasks more tolerable and even fun. These children are often very creative, can easily make others laugh, and have great potential for making a living in some line of entertainment, or professional speaking or training.

REDIRECTED CLOWNING AND SHOW-OFF BEHAVIOR:

Acknowledge their talent and help them see how it could work for them in the future. Structure opportunities for these children to entertain the group or lead in creative activities. Make these opportunities contingent on cooperative behavior. Teach them how entertainers must have respect for their audiences by not demanding attention at inappropriate times.

Disrespectful behavior can hide boldness and daring

As irritating and unacceptable as disrespectful behavior is, it can also be indicative of a strong personality and the ability to push forward even when confronted by a superior force. Disrespectful people are not easily intimidated. They are naturally suspicious of authority and will confront others even at great risk to themselves. Throughout history, individuals with these character traits have been able to expose corruption, challenge unscrupulous leaders and act on behalf of disadvantaged people.

REDIRECTED DISRESPECTFUL BEHAVIOR:

Since this behavior usually elicits a strong reaction from most adults, be careful to distinguish between the unacceptable behavior and the underlying character strength. To acknowledge the strengths of a child or adolescent who acts disrespectfully is not to condone their disrespectful behavior. On the contrary, it gives you the chance to discuss how the underlying traits of boldness and daring can be used positively. Most importantly—model respectful behavior.

Require these children to define who and what it is that they respect. Tell them that it is not enough to disdain authority, they must be able to propose an alternative. Place them in leadership roles where they must become the authority. Create projects that require boldness and daring. Help them request and plan an interview with a powerful official in which they must discuss and plan how to right a wrong. Be creative.

Argumentative behavior can hide cleverness and quick thinking

An argumentative child or adolescent can be aggravating, but keep in mind that making an effective argument requires the ability to think fast as well as to anticipate what others are thinking, or what they might say next. People with these skills make excellent advocates including legal advocacy. Of course legal advocacy is only one channel for these skills, sales and other forms of business are healthy outlets for the naturally argumentative.

REDIRECTED ARGUMENTATIVE BEHAVIOR:

Argumentative kids are generally in the business of trying to get their own way. Teach these children when it is, and is not, useful to argue. Do not let them argue you out of a position that you have taken, but do structure opportunities for them to argue with other students even if it has to be done in a role-playing situation. Make these opportunities contingent on their refraining from inappropriate arguing. Help them recognize how satisfactory it can be to argue in the appropriate setting and how useful their natural talents can be when used properly.

Apathetic behavior can hide natural objectivity

Some people get very angry with apathetic kids because they are so difficult to encourage or motivate. They appear not to care about anything, including their own future, but this is usually not the case. On the contrary, these kids are often hurting deeply. The apathetic behavior hides a great deal of emotional energy as well as pain. Apathetic kids are just naturally gifted at being able to detach themselves from their own feelings, to see the world objectively, and to react without emotions. These people make excellent emergency room personnel, ambulance and rescue workers, and crisis management professionals. They can do what needs to be done even in the most emotionally intense situations.

REDIRECTED APATHETIC BEHAVIOR:

Tell these kids that you can't believe they don't really care about themselves or others. Be careful not to say that you know what they are thinking or feeling. Just let them know that you have faith that at some level they want to be successful and you want to help them. Try to find out what they **do** care about (even if it seems frivolous), and give them opportunities to talk about it, or show them how whatever you are trying to teach applies to their interests. In short, when they show no interest, you act interested.

Predict positive futures for them. Beware of the tendency to the opposite. Tell them that you can imagine them doing the kind of work mentioned above and why. If at all possible, give them opportunities to interact with professionals in this kind of work. Consider outings or field trips to places where this kind of work is done

When they show no interest, you act interested.

Intervention Strategies

Often the first response to a child's difficult or defiant behavior is to punish the child. The tendency is to believe that what is really needed is some new, clever and more effective form of punishment. The problem with this theory is that most punishment methods simply do not work. They may make you feel like you've done something, and they make the child temporarily miserable, but they rarely cause children to change their behavior in the long run.

One reason punishment often doesn't work is that for punishment to be effective children must be able to think in terms of the future. They have to say to themselves, "I better not do this because if I do, I will be punished and I won't like that." This thought process requires them to project themselves mentally into the future, and many are unable to do so (see Interior Landscapes). Also, punishment does not teach appropriate behavior, effective decision-making skills, or the concept of personal choice and responsibility.

Self-control, which is the ability to manage one's own behavior in a positive effective manner, is a learned skill. Many difficult children have not been taught these skills. The goal of any disciplinary action or intervention must be to **teach,** not to punish. As much as we'd like to believe it, punishment doesn't teach positive behavior. *Effective interventions teach or model personal behavior management skills.* The following is a list of strategies which can be used to encourage the development of self-control, cooperation, courtesy and personal responsibility.

Make sure all the limits and guidelines for appropriate behavior are well known.

(See "Remember to Keep It S-I-M-P-L-E")

All kids need to know exactly what is expected of them and where they stand at all times. Be sure you communicate that you expect them to show self-control, cooperation and courtesy and exactly what will and will not be tolerated. If you haven't clearly defined what you consider acceptable behavior, stop and do not proceed with any other agenda with the children in your care until you have done so.

🍎 *Make sure the consequences for negative behavior are clearly defined.*

As much as possible make sure that children know what will happen if they misbehave and that they have the choice to cooperate or act out. They just have to be prepared to accept the consequences of their choices.

🍎 *Be careful of your own agenda. Know your goal.*

Be clear about the goal of your intervention strategy. Make sure the goal is to get the child to comply or cooperate, not just acknowledge that you are right or more powerful, and that they are wrong. Children are very sensitive to motives, and difficult children will react strongly and negatively to efforts to control their behavior, which are motivated solely by a need to prove that you are more powerful.

Also, remember that the only **practical** reason to respond to difficult behavior is to **teach** children appropriate, healthy behavior. If you find yourself feeling a need to prove your own power or authority for the sake of letting them "know who's boss" or to reassure yourself that you are in control, then stop. Take time out for you. Power struggles for the sake of proving who has the power will only drain your energy and have little positive effect on anyone's behavior.

🍎 *Be respectful! Model, Model, Model.*

Difficult children will often mirror your attitude and manner of communicating with them. They do not view **any** behavior as strictly the prerogative of adults. If you want them to be respectful of you and of their peers you must model respectful behavior.

🍎 *Create future.*

Help the child envision a positive future. Say things like: "I can imagine you doing _____ when you grow up." "You are so creative!" "You have a lot of energy." or "I bet you'll end up being _____." Be careful that the future you help them create is **positive**. Don't say things like "You're going to end up a bum if you don't...."

Help them imagine themselves earning a living. Help them understand how their negative behavior would be viewed in the work place, i.e., "If you do that when you get a job, you would be fired." Tell them that part of your job is to prepare them to be successful in the world when they grow up or finish school. You, therefore, CANNOT tolerate behavior that would not be tolerated in the work place.

🍎 Keep your perspective.

Avoid generalizing ("You always..." or "You'll never...") the behavior or making a small issue into a large problem. Parents sometimes have a tendency to make every issue a big issue. This leaves them with few resources when it becomes necessary to respond to the serious defiance, which could result in the child or adolescent being seriously injured or hurt.

🍎 Ignore some behavior (for a short time).

Some negative behavior is best ignored initially, or until you can choose the best time to address the issue. Waiting until you can deal with an issue properly can send a clear message to the child that you are not going to allow him or her to take control of the situation. Make brief eye contact with them to let them know that you are aware of their behavior, but you are in charge of your time, not them. If the behavior begins to escalate, you can say, "I'll be with you in a minute" as though they were waiting customers. Do not use this strategy for a lengthy period of time. Some difficult behavior will even stop when the message becomes clear that the child is not going to take over simply by acting out.

🍎 Use the Socratic method.

As often as possible, whenever you want to call attention to unacceptable behavior, give a command or reprimand, ask a question instead. Say for example: "Excuse me, what are you doing?" "Excuse me, what did we discuss?" "Is this what you are supposed to be doing?"

Do not ask "why" questions like, "Why are you doing this?" or "Why did you do that?" Difficult children rarely if ever know why they do what they are doing. "What" questions help make children more aware of their behavior. It also calls their attention to how their behavior is impacting others and gives them a chance to change their behavior without being directed to do so.

🍎 Listen to the child's story.

Sometimes children have a clear idea of why they have done something unacceptable. Give them a chance to explain when possible. Do not argue with their reasoning. Just restate what you understand them to say, then acknowledge their thinking. This is not the same as agreeing or approving of their choices. After they have been heard, you can respond with your perspective and decision regarding consequences.

🍎 Acknowledge their point of view.

A key element of any conflict resolution is to acknowledge everyone's point of view. You only have to say "I understand that you believe ...." This does not mean that you are agreeing with their point of view.

🍎 Identify and match their pace.

When a child is extremely upset and you are trying to get them to calm down or back off from a confrontation, adjust the speed and rate of your speech to match the child's speed and rate of speech. Make sure your voice stays calm and firm, but speak quickly if they are speaking in a pressured or rapid fashion.

The same is true if the child is slow speaking and/or moving. Slow your pace to meet the child's. This strategy works much like trying to catch up to someone walking away from you in order to tell them something. Matching a verbal pace has much the same effect as trying to talk to someone who is walking. If you want them to hear you, you have to walk at their pace. For the communication to take place you have to get into the rhythm of their verbal stride. Getting into the verbal stride with an emotionally upset child enhances the possibility of being heard and understood, and of course, of getting the response you want.

🍎 Speak softly.

Lower your voice instead of raising it, especially when you are annoyed and things seem to be getting out of control. Beware—the tendency when **we** are upset or frustrated with difficult kids is to let our voice rise or even start yelling. *It is much more effective to speak softly, firmly and emphatically.* Use a firm, slow, no-nonsense but non-threatening tone. A great deal of authority is communicated in the tone and volume of your voice, not just the words.

For communication to take place you have to get into the rhythm of their verbal stride. Getting into the verbal stride with an emotionally upset child enhances the possibility of being heard and understood, and of course, of getting the response you want.

Beware of body language—theirs and yours.

A child's body language can indicate the likelihood of effective communication. If he or she appears angry, hostile or agitated, it is best to direct your actions toward getting the child to calm down. Acknowledge their "apparent" feelings before you attempt to get them to alter their behavior.

Kids watch adults. They are keenly aware of your mood and attitude. Be extremely careful that your body language, including hand gestures, are non-threatening. Remember that 70% of what you communicate is communicated **before** you open your mouth.

Choose your stance and location carefully.

Go to the disruptive child. Do not get too close too quickly, but do not talk to them from across the room. Keep your eyes at a level with the child's eyes whenever possible. Squat down rather than lean over a disruptive child. Choose a firm, solid but non-threatening posture.

Be aware of personal space.

Do not get into a child's personal space unless absolutely necessary, and do not let them get into yours. Many difficult kids are not aware of other people's space and have to be taught to respect personal space. Others are extremely sensitive to their own personal space and will feel very threatened if you get too close. This is a typical response of abused children.

Ask permission to gently touch.

Sometimes a gentle touch can calm a child down, but always ask a child if it is okay to touch them. Not all children respond well to a reassuring touch. Some can have an extremely adverse reaction. Often troubled children and adolescents have had very bad experiences with touch. Also, keep in mind that some schools have rules prohibiting any form of touch. *Beware: Never touch children or adolescents when they or you are angry.* (See STRATEGIES TO BE AVOIDED.)

Other children crave physical affection, and occasionally they will feel like they have to get in trouble to get it. Try not to let this happen. It is okay to reassure children who have gotten themselves in trouble that they are still loved or cared about and that it is only their negative behavior that is unacceptable. It isn't in their best interests to let negative consequences be the first step in getting hugs and kisses. It will have a tendency to undermine the process of giving consequences for negative behavior.

🍎 Articulate effective thinking. (See GUIDELINE #2 on page 51.)

Difficult children rarely have the ability to calm themselves down or make a good decision when they are upset or agitated. Healthy children and adults are able to communicate with themselves in ways which help them get out of intense feelings and into effective thinking modes. Difficult children can't do this. To teach them this vitally important thinking and coping skill, you can walk them through the thinking process when they are angry or upset.

Say clearly and concisely what you want the children to say to themselves to calm themselves down and begin to think. This is not the same as telling children what to do. Say, for instance, "You can calm down now. You can back off. We can work this out. You can take a deep breath." **Do not** say, "Calm down now. Back off. Stop yelling." If you are commanding instead of coaching them on what to say to themselves, they probably will not respond well. Trying to command an angry or agitated child into appropriate behavior often causes the child's behavior to escalate. It can be helpful to think about what you say to yourself when you are upset, and then use those words with the child.

🍎 Go to the big picture.

Help them see how their behavior affects the entire group or family, and other's perceptions of them. You may think this is obvious to the child, *but many difficult kids are unable to mentally observe their own behavior.*

🍎 Outline choices—theirs and yours.

Explain the child's choices and the consequences of those choices. Explain your choices. Help the children understand that negative behavior is a choice which carries with it negative consequences, and you will choose to make sure they experience the consequences of their choices. This process requires up-front time which means that you have to take the time right in the beginning of your work with difficult kids to decide what the rules and consequences will be. This makes it possible for you to **respond** instead of **react** when rules are broken and you get a defiant response when you need and expect cooperation.

Say clearly and concisely what you want the children to say to themselves to calm themselves down and begin to think. This is not the same as telling children what to do.

Children and adolescents (even adults) are far more receptive to listening to you discuss the importance of self-control, courtesy or cooperation when you use stories or metaphors to make your point.

If you have never taken the time to set up clearly defined rules and consequences, it is not too late to start. Children need to understand that they are free to choose to comply with the rules and structure of your home or classroom, or face the consequences of non-compliance. This is the only way to teach them responsibility for their own behavior and take you out of the role of the police officer. It is up to you to enforce the standards and consequences you set up but you are not responsible for their choices. They are.

Unless you are dealing with your own small child in your own home, it is important to remember the you cannot **make** the child do what you want. You **can** lead a child into a positive choice, and you can make certain the child experiences appropriate and immediate consequences for negative behavior.

🍎 Affirm their ability to make a good choice.

This is especially important when you have walked a child through the thinking process, outlined their choices and helped them see the future as it relates to their choices. Express confidence that they can and will make a good choice.

🍎 Give them time to make a good choice.

Give the children time to consider their choices and consequences. Once the choices and consequences have been outlined, wait a short time (five to ten seconds) depending on the child's developmental stage. Do not wait long enough for the child to do anything but consider the immediate choices. Do not go over and over their choices while you wait for them to think. Do follow through with consequences.

🍎 Problem solve with them.

Ask children, "What could you have done differently?" or "What else could you do next time?" Help them identify other options or possible solutions to the problem or alternative responses to the situation that may have led them into trouble. This is all too often overlooked.

🍎 Use stories and metaphors.

Children and adolescents (even adults) are far more receptive to listening to you discuss the importance of self-control, courtesy or cooperation when you use stories or metaphors to make your point. You can help them think about their choices or understand the impact of their choices on themselves and others through stories. You can use animal stories, classic stories or stories you make up yourself. You can say, "Remember how Brer Rabbit got stuck to Tar Baby because he lost his temper and hit without thinking."

Use any story or character that you know to be familiar to the child or adolescent. *The Little Engine That Could*, *The Velveteen Rabbit*, Dr. Suess characters are all good examples of effective coping skills for kids of all ages. (See RECOMMENDED READING *Storytelling: An enjoyable and effective tool.*)

Use metaphors in the same way. Let your examples relate to familiar objects, things or people. This takes some of the "heat" out of confrontations as well as making kids more receptive to your message. One very angry adolescent girl was told that her extremely defensive behavior made it seem to others like she had filters in her ears that had been constructed by her parents so that anything anyone said to her went through the filters and came into her head sounding like a criticism. This made it almost impossible for her to believe that anyone really liked or cared about her. After thinking about the "filters in her ears" for a while, she finally said, "I guess you're right about my ears," and that was the beginning of her being able to trust that some people actually liked and approved of her.

🍎 Follow through.

Always follow through immediately with the consequences as stated. It is essential that children have immediate, concrete, here-and-now consequences for negative behavior whenever possible. Delayed consequences waste time and energy!

🍎 Consider time out as an immediate consequence.

Time out can be an effective consequence depending on the child and the circumstances. A time-out space or room is advisable for most settings when working with difficult kids. For time out to be effective, it must be used appropriately which means, consistently (every time), for fairly short times (about one minute per year of age), with proper supervision, and immediately following a specific infraction. Delayed use of time out is useless at best and increases negative behavior.

If time out is used, make certain children are absolutely clear about what choice **they** made that caused them to be placed in time out before they go to the time-out area. Any further discussion of the situation should be discussed **after** they have served their time. Do not talk to them about the issue that caused them to be placed in time out while they are in time out. This defeats the purpose of time out. (See *Time Out: Abuses and Effective Uses* by Jane Nelsen and Stephen Glenn for a simple but comprehensive guide to the use of time out as a disciplinary tool.)

🍎 Encourage them when they make a bad decision.

Children need to be reassured that a bad decision and/or choice is not necessarily an indication of future failure

Children need to be reassured that a bad decision and/or choice is not necessarily an indication of future failure. Say things like, "You're a smart person and next time, I'm confident you'll make a different choice." Do not say, "You should have known better." This will just make them decide to prove to you that they do not care about the consequences.

🍎 Make them do writing and thinking exercises.

Difficult children need to learn how their behavior affects others. One effective consequence for children old enough to write is to make a writing assignment. Require them to write a thoughtful paper on the impact of their behavior on others, the group or the class. Be creative. Make it so they have to think a little bit. For example: "How would it be if there were no rules against hitting, stealing, coming late to class, treating other people rudely, etc.?" Be certain that some privilege is withheld until the writing assignment is completed. Do not be concerned about writing skills as much as thoughtful ideas. Do not have them write meaningless sentences. The only reason to do this exercise is to encourage them to think about their behavior.

🍎 Conference with the child.

Remember that all difficult behavior has a root cause and getting to the root of the needs and goals of the child's behavior is the best chance of eliminating the negative behaviors. Therefore, whenever possible find a time and place to speak quietly and privately with difficult children both before and after disciplinary action has taken place.

First ask them what they are doing and what their understanding of the rules are. It is important to get their interpretation of their own behavior. Beware of asking the "why" they did what they did. They will probably shrug or say "I don't know." You can help them figure out their own behavior by guessing what might be going on with them, but be sure and do this carefully, respectfully and with an open attitude.

Remember, you cannot possibly be certain what was going on in their heads. They don't even know, and, to be sure, the reasons are fairly complex. Once you have some idea of what might have prompted the difficult behavior, ask them what they intend to do in the future. Tell them exactly what you want them to do, and that you are confident they can and will meet your expectations.

Conference with parents.

Whenever possible have your first conference with a difficult child's parents before a problem arises. Beware of your judgments about parents. Many parents of difficult children are struggling to understand their children and to do the right thing. (See GUIDELINES FOR PARENT/TEACHER CONFERENCES.)

Conference with parents and child together.

When you ask the child to join the parent conference, be especially careful to acknowledge the child's strengths. *Do not expect the parent to side with you against the child. Instead, explain to the child that you want him or her to know exactly what you are saying to his or her parents and visa versa.* Treat the child as respectfully as you do the parents.

Humor them.

Gentle teasing and a humorous approach is probably the most effective intervention strategy available to teachers. Humor is the shortest distance between two people. Be careful to make fun **with** a child but NEVER make fun **of** a child!

Affirm they can do it. Teach affirmation.

Always assert your confidence that the child can and will make a good choice, but recognize that he or she needs help in making positive changes. Teach children to encourage themselves by using positive affirmations.

Many children and adults are defeated by their own self-talk. Help children learn to say encouraging things to themselves, making sure all encouraging phrases are positive. Teach them to say, "I can do this." "I can stay on task." or "I am a smart person." instead of "I won't screw up again." or "I'm not stupid." "I will not..." or "I am not..." phrases just reinforce the negative thoughts and feelings they are trying to override.

Tell them exactly what you want them to do, and that you are confident they can and will meet your expectations.

INEFFECTIVE STRATEGIES
(Strategies That Will Backfire)

Some behavior intervention strategies commonly used will have a negative rebound effect. Adults who use the strategies described below often meet with frustration and a defiant, rather than compliant, child response. Remember that personal energy depletion and increased stress will sometimes lead to use of ineffective strategies. Use your personal energy wisely and avoid these behavior management pitfalls.

Ridicule

Many difficult children carry inside themselves inner cores of shame and guilt related to past traumas or failures. Ridicule or interventions which embarrass the child will trigger those feelings, and most certainly will fail to motivate the child to comply or cooperate. Always avoid embarrassing a child and never, never ridicule. **Note:** It is okay to respectfully point out when a child's behavior is embarrassing you, the class or him/herself. No one likes to be embarrassed, and difficult children need to be reminded how their behavior affects others.

Invalidating feelings or thoughts

Never say, "You shouldn't feel that way." It is okay for kids to feel however they choose. It is **not** okay for them to **do** whatever they choose. Help them understand the difference, but do not put them down for making bad decisions or having thoughts or feelings with which you disagree. A simple "I'm sorry you feel that way" will often suffice. Remember it is okay to hate algebra or math, but it is not okay to flunk it.

Put-downs

Never insult or put down a child even in jest. Do not allow kids to do that to one another. **Make respectful behavior the standard in your home, classroom or work place.** Never excuse this behavior by saying, "Children are just naturally cruel." Children are **not** naturally cruel; they learn cruelty if we are not careful to teach them kindness.

🍎 Sarcasm

Most difficult kids do not understand the nuances of sarcasm. Children who are able to understand the double message that sarcasm sends will react and feel put-down or ridiculed. Children who do not understand will just feel confused or stupid. In either case, no good will come out of it. Be certain your goal is to gain cooperation and compliance, not just to get a reaction.

🍎 Threats and ultimatums

Threats are useless. They are usually inflammatory. Rely instead on the rules and the consequences. It is effective to point out the consequences of inappropriate and disruptive behavior. It is ineffective to use threatening words, tones or gestures. They will most certainly have a negative rebound effect with difficult children.

Many difficult kids will almost invite a threatening response. Don't get caught up in this fruitless struggle. Stick with the limits and consequences you have outlined. There is a difference between a threat and a promise. You can promise to follow-through with already defined consequences. Do so.

🍎 Nagging and criticism

Usually nagging is an indication that the adult (teacher, parent, childcare worker) has taken responsibility for the child's behavior. It keeps the adults pushing and prodding instead of allowing the child to fail or make a bad choice and face the necessary consequences. Nagging is a great energy drain and stressor—for the nagger as well as the nagged. Don't allow yourself to get caught up in it.

Criticism only points out faults. It does not teach or encourage effective and positive behavior in anyone. It makes people feel bad which means they do not improve, but they get worse. They do not do well in managing their own behavior, cooperating with others, or being considerate of other people. In short, criticism is a waste.

🍎 Disrespectful interruptions

Do not jump into the middle of their story with an angry response. Listen to the children without interruption. If you have to postpone

Threats are useless. They are usually inflammatory. Rely instead on the rules and the consequences.

117

hearing them until later, tell them that you are willing to hear them at such and such a time, but for now you need them to do whatever is necessary. Be sure to go back and listen to what they have to say.

🍎 Commanding children to do what you want.

Commands such as "Sit down, now" or "Be quiet" can sometimes be effective with younger children in a crisis situation, or in the case of escalating defiance, but should be avoided in the normal course of communication. It is essential for adults to model respectful behavior at all times which means stating directives in the form of firm but respectful requests. "Will you please sit down, now?" or "Please, stop talking now."

🍎 Power struggles.

Power struggles are unnecessary when the limits, boundaries and consequences have been clearly laid out. Remember that you do not have to prove anything except that you have self-control, and the authority as the adult in charge.

Power struggles are about emotional conflict. Anger and hostility met with anger and hostility will only make a situation worse. Stay cool and model cool-headed thinking. Rely on structure and consequences to remove yourself from a power struggle. Tell children that while you may not be able to **make** them do what they must do, you can and will make certain that they experience the consequences of their choices.

CRISIS INTERVENTION IN THE CLASSROOM

More and more educators are experiencing daily disturbances in the classroom due to disruptive behavior. Often the disruptive behavior reaches crisis levels. A behavior crisis is defined as any behavior which is dangerous to the child, the teacher or other children. It can also be any behavior that is sufficiently disruptive to make it necessary for instruction to be halted completely until the behavior can be stopped or an appropriate intervention implemented. The following suggestions can help minimize the stress and reduce the energy expended in dealing with behavior crisis.

Define the behaviors which will not be tolerated in the classroom.

Make sure students are made aware of exactly what behavior will not be tolerated. Be aware that verbally aggressive or threatening behavior will often lead to physically aggressive behavior and should be considered equally unacceptable.

As much as possible define the consequences students will experience if they participate in a behavior crisis.

It is very important to outline precisely what the consequences will be for creating or participating in a behavior crisis **before** any crisis occurs. Do not be afraid that discussing unacceptable behavior and its consequences will stimulate some students to test the limits. The reverse is more likely to happen. Students tend to test limits more often when either the limits or the consequences are not clearly defined.

Always have a backup person and plan.

Letting the children in your care know that you are prepared to deal with disruptive behavior quickly and efficiently will minimize the likelihood that you will need to do so. When working in settings which

Much the same as
a fire evacuation
plan is a necessary
part of prudent
classroom
management,
a crisis intervention
plan should be
practiced on
a periodic basis.

require you to attend to many children at once such as schools or day care centers, it is best to have a crisis management plan in place in the event that one child becomes dangerously out of control. Much the same as a fire evacuation plan is a necessary part of prudent classroom management, a crisis intervention plan should be **practiced** on a periodic basis. New children coming in should be made aware of the plan.

🍎 Appoint someone to go for help.

If there is no way to alert others directly from the classroom, then make certain someone goes for help immediately and make sure that person knows who they are **before** the crisis occurs. Appoint a runner and rotate the appointment if necessary.

🍎 Teach the children that they share in the responsibility for maintaining order in the classroom.

Explain to the class members that they must choose to be part of the problem or part of the solution when the class is in a crisis management plan.

🍎 Make certain the class or group members know what they are to do.

Class members should be told exactly what they should do while the teacher is responding to the crisis. This should be discussed and practiced with the class.

🍎 Give a verbal signal to the class before you go to the disruptive student or students.

Alert the class to go into the crisis management response. Simply say something like, "Class you know what to do." or "Everyone, move." Moving everyone away from the disruptive child or children sends a clear signal that the disturbance will not be allowed to spread.

🍎 Acknowledge and address the feelings.

To get someone to calm down it is necessary to let them know that you recognize and understand their feelings. Say, "I can see that you are upset (angry) and I understand."

🍎 Acknowledgment is not agreement.

To say that you understand is not to say that you **agree** with what a hostile student is saying. You are only saying that you understand his or her **perception** on what is happening.

🍎 Perceptions of reality are reality to an emotionally aroused person.

Angry person's feelings are very real to them and denial of their reality, as they perceive it, will increase their anger.

🍎 Beware of your body language.

Make sure your body language reflects calm and balance. Be careful not to lean over or into an angry person. Keep your hands relaxed and at your sides.

🍎 Observe carefully.

Watch the body language of the angry student or students. Body language is as important as verbal language in judging the level of threat or hostility of an angry person. When the words and the body language do not match, believe the body.

🍎 Do not touch an angry or hostile student.

Remember that perceptions are distorted when people are angry. Touching an angry student can easily be perceived as a threatening gesture by the student and result in your someone else's getting hurt.

HOW TO DEFUSE AN ANGRY CHILD
🍎 Remain calm.

Keeping your composure is essential. While you are dealing with the angry person, do not let your anger surface or take over. Give yourself an opportunity to process your own emotions **after** the incident is over.

🍎 Go to the disruptive child.

Do not try to deal effectively with an angry child from across the room. Get close enough to the child to make certain he or she knows that he or she has your full and undivided attention. Go to the student but do not get into his or her personal space.

Angry person's feelings are very real to them and denial of their reality, as they perceive it, will increase their anger.

🍎 Be careful of your stance.

Stay aware of your body language keeping an open and balanced stance. The goal is to look self-assured, NOT threatening. Do not use threatening words or gestures.

🍎 Communicate a reassuring and empathetic attitude.

Reassure the child that you can work things out and that you are listening to his or her story.

🍎 Listen carefully.

Pay very close attention to what the child is saying, and what he or she appears to be feeling.

🍎 Restate what you have heard them say with empathy.

Repeat back to the angry child what you think he or she is saying and feeling. Say, "I can see that you are angry, (say this without judgment) because..." Or say, "I can see that you're upset and I want to hear what you have to say."

🍎 Use respectful language and a firm but non-threatening tone.

Choose your words carefully. Do not say anything insulting, hostile, threatening or patronizing. Treat the angry child like you would an angry colleague. Use a firm, but non-threatening, tone of voice.

🍎 Keep reassuring the child until he or she begins to calm down.

Tell the child, "I'm sure we can work this out. Let's go outside and discuss this." Try to get the child to sit if he or she is standing. Try to get him or her away from the group.

🍎 Predict the future.

Outline the children's choices and consequences. Help them see where their actions will lead and how it will benefit them to back off and calm down. Outline what your response will be if they are unwilling to back off or settle down and how you would like to work things out without having to get others involved.

🍎 Walk them through the thinking process.

Say the words to the children you would like them to be saying to themselves if they were calm and thinking clearly. Help them bring themselves down emotionally. This includes telling them that they **can** calm down and back off. Reassure them that you are certain they don't really want to deal with the consequences (be specific about the pending consequences) and that they can act in their own best interests.

🍎 Praise and acknowledge their ability to make a good decision.

Praise and acknowledgment are great defusers. Sometimes it can be very calming to appeal to an angry person's strengths while reassuring them that you know they can and will make a good decision.

🍎 Give them time to make a decision.

Do not try to rush the process. Tell them that you will give them some time to decide.

🍎 Be sure and give the child an out.

Be sure there is a benefit to the child for calming down and backing off. Let them know that if they respond to your request before you have to call for help or help arrives, then the consequences will be far less than if they have to be removed from the room.

🍎 Do not take insults or abusive language personally.

Refer to WHEN A CONFERENCE BECOMES A CONFLICT. Whether you are dealing with your child, a parent, student or colleague, do not allow yourself to let the reactions of a hostile person become an indictment of your character. You are in charge of you, not them.

🍎 When all else fails, back off!

It is always better to back off if the child gets threatening or refuses to comply with your requests or reassurances. Keep in mind the only thing you have to prove is that you have self-control. **Backing off will make you look smart, not weak.** Set the example for rational thinking and behavior.

*Do not say,
"Calm down."
Say instead,
"You are a smart
person. I know
you can make
a good decision."*

🍎 If a punch is thrown or physical combat is taking place, get the police.

Most conflicts can be handled with a cool head, and the above outlined step-by-step approach, but if hostilities escalate, DO NOT TRY TO BREAK UP A FIGHT! DO NOT TOUCH A VIOLENT PERSON! Use your voice and verbal commands to attempt to get violent students to back off. If they do not respond, do not physically intervene without proper self-defense training. Get help. If you have on-campus police, then SEND FOR THE POLICE.

Be aware that you can be held liable if a child/student gets hurt in a physical struggle with you, even if you are only trying to help save another child/student. Stay out of the fight. It is far too easy to get hurt, and no good will come of your being hurt.

Many parents feel intimidated and defensive before anything is even said. Your first goal is to reassure parents that you are not going to criticize them or their child.

If possible, plan a parent conference BEFORE a problem arises.

This helps build positive rapport between parents and teachers and reassures parents that you are committed to helping their child be successful.

Find a way to put parents at ease.

Small talk can serve a valuable purpose. It can establish common ground. Usually even very different people can agree on some trivial matter like the weather. Beginning with some kind of agreement will set a positive tone.

Many parents feel intimidated and defensive before anything is even said. Your first goal is to reassure parents that you are not going to criticize them or their child. It isn't necessary or advisable to be critical even when you must tell them their child is not doing well.

Always acknowledge the child's strengths.

Even the most difficult child has strengths, and all parents want to hear positive things about their child. (See CAN YOU IDENTIFY THE CHILD'S STRENGTHS?) Often you can discover their strengths by looking at their most irritating quality. When you can't find something positive to say, try saying "You have a very interesting child." No doubt that statement is true.

Be an active listener.

Make certain parents feel like they have been heard. Paraphrase what you hear them saying. Say, "Let me be sure I understand what you've said." This does not mean that you are agreeing with what they are saying, but you must let them know you have heard and respect their point of view.

Ask parents for their suggestions or feedback.

Obviously parents know things about their child that you do not. Always be sure and ask parents how they think you can help.

You may get some valuable information to say nothing of giving them the message that you value their input.

🍎 Keep a solution-oriented attitude.

Keep your focus on what will help and not on what is wrong. It is easy to outline what is wrong. It is another matter to find creative solutions.

🍎 Be careful of your language. Avoid the word "problem" whenever possible.

Encourage yourself and parents to think creatively. Think in terms of "opportunity" instead of "problem." Within every problem lies the opportunity to be creative and effective in helping a child succeed.

🍎 Always ask if you can make suggestions.

Even if you are certain what would help, ask first if you may make a suggestion before offering advice.

🍎 Encourage parents to communicate with you.

Urge parents to feel free to talk to you any time. It can even be helpful if they feel comfortable to let you know when something at home may be affecting their child's school performance.

🍎 When you are particularly anxious about a conference, rehearse with a colleague.

If you are worried about how a conference may go, give yourself a chance to calm down by talking about your concerns with a colleague. Be careful not to let your pre-conference turn into a gripe session about the child or the parents. Keep your focus on how you want it to turn out, not on what is wrong with everyone involved or on your fears of being criticized.

🍎 Be kind to yourself. Acknowledge your hard work, even when it seems like no one else does.

Don't be too disappointed if parents don't acknowledge your genuine concern and hard work on their child's behalf. Sometimes they are overwhelmed with their own lives. It is important to tell yourself that you are

It is important to tell yourself that you are working hard and doing your best for their child, even if you don't hear that from parents or supervisors

working hard and doing your best for their child, even if you don't hear that from parents or supervisors. Practice supporting yourself, especially when others don't.

WHEN A CONFERENCE BECOMES A CONFLICT

Whether a conflict develops with a parent, a child, a colleague or a supervisor, the following guidelines will help keep the conflict from escalating. They will also enhance the chance of achieving a mutually agreeable resolution. Keep in mind they are guidelines for handling **yourself**, and responding effectively to the other person NOT handling them so they will do what you want.

🍎 Stay calm.

If you feel your temper getting ready to flair or your eyes starting to tear up (typical reactions to hostility), then take some deep breaths. Gently push your chair back, or step back just an inch or so and say to yourself "Be cool." or "I'm okay." Don't tell yourself or them to "calm down." Often telling yourself (or anyone else for that matter) to calm down only makes matters worse.

🍎 Remember that you are in charge of your self-esteem.

You can keep your own defenses down by remembering that you do not **need** their approval or acknowledgment of your hard work. Your goal needs to establish mutual respect, not necessarily agreement.

🍎 Listen carefully.

Look like you're listening, not like you are simply waiting to defend yourself. The appearance of sincere listening is as important as actually listening.

🍎 Acknowledge their feelings not just their concerns.

Let them know you have some understanding of how they feel. Say, "I understand that you feel angry (worried, offended, anxious) and are concerned about your child." This does not mean you agree with their perspective. It only means that you have heard and understand their position.

If you skip this step, the communication *will* break down.
Empathetic listening and responding is vital to any conflict resolution.

Focus on
any mutually
agreeable goal...
Say, "We both
want your son
or daughter to be
successful," or
"I'm sure we
can work this
out somehow."

🍎 Paraphrase what you heard them say.

Be sure they believe you understand what they have said before you counter their argument. Restate what you have heard them say, and then ask, "Is that correct. Is that what you are saying?" If they say, "No, it isn't," then try again.

🍎 Be sure to state your concerns in the form of an "I" message.

State your concerns in the form of an "I" message. Say, "I feel bad that you think I've been unfair," or "I feel frustrated that I can't help you understand why I made the decisions I have." This is much less inflammatory than saying, "You don't understand," or "You aren't listening to what I'm saying."

People who become defensive do not listen. When serious disagreements are in progress, statements that begin with "you" have a tendency to put people on the defense. Instead, calm folks down. Keep in mind step one—stay calm. Be reassuring to yourself and them. You can't think well enough to choose your words if you are angry.

🍎 Reassure them that you want to work things out.

Focus on any mutually agreeable goal even with major differences in how you will achieve the goal. Say, "We both want your son or daughter to be successful," or "I'm sure we can work this out somehow." This gives the message that you are willing to work at a solution, and not just insist on your own way.

🍎 Ask what they want you to do.

Do not assume you know what is really causing the conflict. Ask them to tell you exactly what they want. Sometimes this can cut through a great deal of arguing and hostility, and sometimes you can do what they want, once you are clear about what it is. Knowing exactly what everyone wants also increases the possibility of coming up with an acceptable compromise.

🍎 When no agreement seems likely, agree to disagree.

Sometimes just acknowledging that you cannot agree on a solution to the difficulty is a way to establish the only common ground possible. Say,

"For now, can we just agree to disagree," or "Maybe we can find a way to resolve this later." Sometimes time and distance can reveal hidden possibilities for solutions.

How to respond to criticism

If parents criticize your work with their child:

- Redo the steps for dealing with a conflict—reiterate the acknowledgment of their feelings.

- Explain your actions or decisions, but do not be drawn into defending yourself.

You may need to **explain** yourself but **defending** yourself only makes things worse. There is a significant difference between explaining and defending. Explaining helps others to understand your rationale. Defending usually makes them more hostile and aggressive. It is helpful to say, "I would be glad to explain why I made the decision I did." It is **not** helpful to say "I have not been unfair or biased against your child because he/she did this or that, etc.," "I did not...." "I am not...." or "You are wrong...."—especially without listening and reflecting back on what you have heard. These are all ways of defending yourself. They send a clear message that you are insecure about yourself or your position, and that you are not listening.

● Acknowledge their criticism.

Let them know that you have heard their concerns or accusations. Say, "I understand that you think that I...." Ignoring or defending will often increase an already hostile reaction.

● Ask again what they would have you do.

Ask parents exactly what they want you to do. Remember, you do not have to agree to do it, but you can sometimes deflect or absorb a great deal of criticism by simply asking, "What is it that you want me to do?"

● Tell them if you can or cannot do what they ask.

Tell parents if you can do what they want. If not, offer an alternative. Do not "just say no." Parents are looking for some kind of cooperation, and a complete refusal to do anything they consider helpful will probably invite more criticism.

> There is a significant difference between explaining and defending. Explaining helps others to understand your rationale. Defending usually makes them more hostile and aggressive.

🍎 Do not get defensive.

The more critical others become, the more tempting it is to get defensive. Stay off the defense. No one can listen and defend at the same time. Remember that you hold title to your self-esteem and no one can make you feel bad about yourself without your cooperation.

🍎 Do not criticize their comments.

Responding to criticism with criticism is never helpful. Even though you feel like telling them they are being unreasonable or unfair, be careful not to counterattack. Remember, when feelings are intense, thinking is impaired and therefore they are not likely to hear and respond to your criticism objectively.

🍎 Go back to the goals for their child.

Your personal goal is to maintain your composure and to keep their focus of the conference on the issue regarding the child, not on the issue of your personal feelings. Go back to the goals of the conference. You can deal with your feelings **after** the conference is ended.

🍎 Emphasize your mutual concerns and goals.

Restate that you both want the child to be successful even if you can't agree on how to achieve that goal.

WHAT TO DO WHEN

SCHOOL PERFORMANCE BEGINS TO SLIP

🍎 *Do not assume they are just being lazy or irresponsible.*

1. Make sure there is no physical or emotional reason for your child's lack of school performance. Has there been a family crisis or trauma? Is the child having problems with friends? Could they be feeling sad or depressed? Could there be a physical reason for the problem? Are they getting enough sleep and exercise? Could it be an eye problem?

2. If you discover something is going on with your child, then discuss his or her feelings and your concerns. Remember, kids cannot always figure out just what they are feeling so don't assume that they don't want to talk about their feelings. Sometimes they just don't know what to say.

3. Seek professional help if you think something might be going on with your child or you have a difficult or frustrating time trying to communicate. Good professional counseling can be very helpful, even when kids don't want to go. In fact, one sign of a good therapist is a person who can put a child or adolescent at ease even when they are very resistant to "talking to a shrink."

🍎 *If you are certain that the only reason for the poor performance is lack of initiative or responsibility:*

1. Be sure and discuss how and why you value a good education. Emphasize the importance and usefulness of gaining knowledge, not just the fact that good jobs are contingent on a good education.

2. Help them imagine how they will feel in the presence of people who are educated when they are not. Kids who do not like or enjoy school rarely think about why being an educated person is important.

3. Calmly discuss your expectations about school performance with your child. Keep in mind that it is your child's responsibility to correct the situation. You can only set guidelines,

You can only set guidelines, outline consequences and provide support. Your child must do the rest.

Be sure your child understands that the choices he or she made are what led to the consequences; i.e., the consequences are not the results of your behavior but the child's.

outline consequences and provide support. **Your child must do the rest.**

4. Express confidence that your child is up to this challenge.

5. Help your child develop a problem-solving plan. (How they will handle the situation differently the next time or how they will study to bring grades up.)

6. Explain your expectations regarding the plan.

7. Discuss the rewards and consequences, for both school and home, if expectations are or are not met. Make sure your child clearly understands all consequences before the plan is implemented.

8. Be careful to make the consequences fit the "crime." Save big consequences for big issues.

9. Make sure there are frequent rewards along the way.

10. Check daily to see if your child is working the plan. If not, only remind him or her of the rewards and consequences. **Resist the temptation to nag.**

11. Remember a hug, a "great going" or a pat on the back can be a powerful reinforcer for good work or good behavior.

12. Be sure the consequences of not following the plan are **always** experienced. Never "let it slide" once a consequence has been defined. Just like hitting a ball with a bat, tennis racket or golf club, **follow through is everything.**

13. If it becomes necessary to follow through with negative consequences, be sure your child understands that the choices he or she made are what led to the consequences; i.e., the consequences are not the results of your behavior but the child's.

14. Keep a positive attitude even if things don't go as well as you had hoped at first. **Remember:** learning a new way to study or better ways to handle problems can be very hard work and takes time and patience. **Be patient with yourself and your child.**

Guidelines for Working with Children or Adolescents with Attention Deficit Disorder

There are many excellent books written on the subject of helping kids with attention deficit disorder. If you are working or living with children who have been diagnosed with this disorder, you will find it beneficial to learn as much as you can to help the child deal with the challenge of ADD. The following are simple guidelines which can help with your interactions with these children. All other guidelines and strategies discussed in the first two sections apply to working with children diagnosed with Attention Deficit Disorder.

Do:

Acknowledge their feelings.

These children often have very intense feelings about everything. Their feelings of frustration and discouragement when they cannot do what is expected of them are also intense. It is important to acknowledge that you understand they have "big" feelings and to help them recognize that *these feelings are okay, but how they act on their feelings may be a problem, because feelings and actions are not the same.*

Affirm their ability to be successful.

Express your confidence in them. Help them believe that you believe in them and their ability to do what they need to do.

Recognize and affirm their strengths.

Call attention to their strengths as often as possible. Many of these kids are very creative and innovative. Even their distractibility can be a strength when it helps them find creative ways to do things or gives them the ability to do more than one thing at a time. (Keep in mind, some career fields absolutely require this skill.)

🍎 Allow them to "own the challenge."

Attention Deficit Disorder is an unfortunate name or description for a set of symptoms or characteristics. No one likes to be labeled "disordered." That is why children need to be helped to reframe the notion of "disorder" to the concept of challenges and limitations. Everyone has limitations.

Kids with ADD need to understand that the characteristics of the disorder, such as difficulty staying focused on task, organizing or attending to a sequence of commands, or motivating themselves without support, are merely challenges that you are confident they will meet successfully. They simply have to learn strategies for dealing effectively with their limitations, and you expect that they will do so.

🍎 Help them create structure.

You can help set up ways to help ADD kids organize their time and their work. **Caution:** this does not mean make yourself responsible for their time management, chores or school work

🍎 Help them to focus on skills.

The ability to organize, set up reminder systems, learn strategies for staying on task, and manage time are all learned skills. ADD kids have to work very hard to learn these skills, and it is most helpful to keep your focus and theirs on the skill-building process and not on the limitation, i.e., their disorganization, distractibility, impulsivity, etc.

🍎 Give them verbal or visual cues.

A cue is a visual sign or gesture, or a one- or two-word signal. It is not a sentence and definitely not a lecture. Find ways to give a "stay on task," "watch your time," or "do it the first time" signal. Signals can help. Lectures never do.

🍎 Expect them to be responsible.

ADD kids can and must learn to be responsible for themselves. Model responsible behavior and talk to them about how important it is to be accountable and dependable.

🍎 Encourage and praise often.

It is so important to stay positive in your attitude and expectations with these kids. Reassure them constantly and acknowledge their smallest successes. Praise is a powerful energizer.

DON'T:
🍎 Do not lecture.

Lectures are useless—burning up your energy while kids tune them out. They may give us the feeling that we have "done something" about some difficult behavior when all we've done is waste time and energy.

🍎 Do not do it for them.

Do not do things for ADD kids that they can do for themselves. It does not communicate that you care or understand their needs. It communicates that you do not have faith in their ability.

🍎 Do not criticize.

Criticism focuses on what's wrong. If you really want improvement, focus on what you want them to do, not what they have done wrong.

🍎 Do not make excuses for them.

Many mothers fall into this trap. They feel so much for their child's struggles and frustrations that they overcompensate for them by explaining away all their irresponsibility or difficult behavior. They say, "Well, you have to understand that he has ADD and really can't...."

This is hurtful to children. It ultimately makes them feel powerless because it prevents them from taking responsibility for themselves. If the reason for behavior is strictly a matter of a disorder, then the person is powerless to do anything about it. It is almost impossible to have any sense of power over any aspect of our lives for which we feel no responsibility. Don't help them make excuses for themselves.

🍎 Do not run interference for them.

This means do not try to protect ADD kids from the consequences of their actions by explaining their behavior and trying to influence teachers,

It is almost impossible to have any sense of power over any aspect of our lives for which we feel no responsibility. Don't help them make excuses for themselves.

coaches or caretakers to make special allowances for difficult or irresponsible behavior.

🍎 Do not expect them to do things your way.

If you are a highly focused, highly organized, goal-oriented, on-task kind of person, it can be very difficult to understand how an ADD person experiences the world. It is easy to believe that ADD kids just need to "get it together." The belief is that they could do things the way you do them if they just tried hard enough. This belief can cause everyone involved to feel like a failure: the adults because they haven't managed to correct the child's behavior and the child because they can't live up to the unrealistic expectations.

🍎 Do not expect them to do things the way a non-ADD person can do them.

As much as it is important to maintain a positive attitude and expectations for these children, it is only bound to cause frustration or even heartache to expect these kids to someday be free of all ADD characteristics, and therefore behave like people who never have had to face the challenges of ADD. Even the most highly skilled ADD adults who have experienced great success never interact in the world like highly focused, highly organized, non-ADD people.

Even the most highly skilled ADD adults who have experienced great success never interact in the world like highly focused, highly organized, non-ADD people.

136

BURNOUT PREVENTION STRATEGIES
Remember to L-A-U-G-H

*A*lways remember in working with difficult children that you are the most important tool that you have. Your healthy mind, body and spirit are the first, last and most important requirements for success in your job.

Throughout this book you have been cautioned to guard your own natural energy supply and to recognize that ineffective strategies can deplete those supplies. Now consider what it takes to stay healthy and energized, and make a commitment to taking care of yourself by using the L-A-U-G-H approach.

LISTEN TO YOUR BODY.

Your body is your friend. It will tell you what you need to take care of yourself, if you listen to it carefully. Unfortunately, most often, we do not listen. We live in a culture that suggests we medicate ourselves at the first sign of pain. Medications can certainly be helpful, but sometimes it is more helpful to recognize that our body is hurting for a reason. Sometimes the pain is a signal for rest, relaxation or play. Sometimes the pain is telling us to let something go, or give ourselves permission to say "no."

Take time to listen quietly to what your body might be saying to you. Do you know where your body feels stress first? Do you respect your body's wisdom? Almost three quarters of a million Americans die each year from heart disease. Many of these deaths could be prevented by simply respecting the body's wisdom and needs. Stop, rest, breathe deeply, take time out. With proper care your body will last a lifetime.

ATTITUDE AND AFFIRMATIONS ENERGIZE.

Energy and attitude are closely tied together. No doubt you have noticed that when you are fatigued, your attitude starts to slip and vice versa. That is why it so important to protect your attitude. It is in your control, but can be easily influenced by others. Stay away from people who make you feel bad. Stay away from people who have nothing good to say. These people may mean well, but their way of coping can be very energy draining to others. It is okay, even wise, to avoid them if you can.

137

Affirm that you are a caring and loving person. Affirm whatever it is that you want for yourself and the children in your care. Affirmations should be part of your on-going self-talk. Just as it is important to watch how you talk to others, it is equally important to be careful of how you talk to yourself. Create simple affirmations for yourself. They will support your attitude and keep your spirits up.

Your attitude reflects your overall response to life, and your response to life can be even more important than what happens to you. You can't always control what happens, but you do have control over your response. A sense of control is important when dealing with stress, and can make a world of difference in terms of the lasting effects of stress. Keep your attitude in your control if you want to protect yourself from fatigue and emotional depletion.

UNDERSTAND YOURSELF AND WHAT GIVES YOU PLEASURE.

Your pleasure is your best source of personal energy replenishment. Notice how good you feel after you've spent time doing something you love. Take time to do the things you love, and be aware that what gives pleasure to one person may feel like work to others. Pleasurable activities only energize you if you enjoy them. If you don't like jogging, don't expect it to energize you just because it has that effect on a friend or spouse. Also, make sure that what you are doing is not just something you think is good for you like exercising, which is good and necessary, but may not be considered pleasurable.

The problem for some people is that it has been so long since they made the time to do fun and enjoyable things, they can't even remember what those things were. If you can't remember what you used to enjoy, think back to your childhood, and go do what you used to like to do as a child. You'll be surprised at how good you will feel.

GIVE YOURSELF A BREAK.

Give yourself permission to do nothing. Just relax. You don't have to be accomplishing something or taking care of someone all the time. There are endless demands on the time of highly responsible people.

Consider time spent in enjoyable pursuits as an investment in your personal health and energy supply.

Sometimes it feels irresponsible to take time out for yourself, your pleasures, or just for goofing off. It isn't. It is a necessary and healthy part of any good self-care strategy.

Consider time spent in enjoyable pursuits as an investment in your personal health and energy supply. Make time each day (at least, each week) to do the things you love to do. Put your fun time and down time at the top of your priority list.

MAKE A HABIT OF TAKING CARE OF YOURSELF.

It can feel very uncomfortable to take time out for yourself if you have long been used to pushing forward with work, chores or other responsibilities all the time. Some people feel guilty or selfish when they first start to put their personal self-care strategies at the top of the priority list. Recognize that these uncomfortable feelings will pass. Once the habit of taking care of yourself is first established, the sense of irresponsibility or selfishness will go away. Habits are changed one day at a time. Keep at it. The rewards are worth it.

ALWAYS REMEMBER TO LAUGH!

All the self-care strategies combine to spell **LAUGH.** Laughter is the most powerful stress management tool of all. Always find something to make you laugh. Laughter improves your immune system, your overall health, your attitude, your performance, your outlook and your pleasure. It is the shortest distance between two people, and the number one successful strategy for working or living with difficult kids.

Laugh and enjoy yourself. Then laugh and enjoy the children in your care. It is the pathway to your success and theirs.

Laughter is the most powerful stress management tool of all. Always find something to make you laugh.

A FINAL WORD ON HOPE...

Hope for the children...
Be gentle, but firm with the children,
for many are wounded
and they have much to learn and far to go.

Hope for yourself...
Be gentle, but firm with yourself,
for sometimes you, too, are hurting,
and must care for yourself
if you are to enjoy the fruits of your labor.

Hope for each other...
Be gentle, but firm with one another,
for we all have hurts and heartaches of our own,
and we must care for each other,
because we have much to learn and far to go.

APPENDIX

COULD THIS ADOLESCENT BE SUICIDAL?

Suicide is the third leading cause of death behind unintentional injury (car accidents) and homicide for young people between the ages of 15-24. In 1992 more teenagers and young adults died from suicide than from cancer, heart disease, AIDS, birth defects, stroke, pneumonia and influenza, and chronic lung disease **combined**, according to the National Center for Prevention and Control of Violence.

Few adults working with this age group are educated about the signs of suicidal risk or what to do if they suspect a teenager is feeling suicidal. Anyone working with adolescents should be aware of the following signs:

Suicide Risk Signals

- Verbal suicide threats.

- Previous suicide threats or attempts.

- Personality changes (unusual withdrawal, aggression or moodiness).

- High risk behavior (alcohol or drug use, speeding and dangerous play).

- Depression (changes in normal appetite, sleep disturbances, sudden drop in school performance, angry outbursts or tearfulness).

- Loss of interest in friends, hobbies, school, etc.

- Final arrangements (making a will, giving away personal items, suicidal poetry or written communication).

- Increased use of alcohol or drug/substance abuse.

- Truancy or delinquent behavior (scrapes with the law, shoplifting).

- Recent emotional loss or disappointment (break up with boy/girl friend, death of a family member or friend, academic or sports failure).

- Extreme family conflict (physical or sexual abuse going on at home, drug addicted parents, "hopeless" life situations).

- Unkempt personal appearance.

MYTHS AND FACTS ABOUT SUICIDE

MYTH: People who say they are going to commit suicide never really do.

FACT: Most people who commit suicide do tell someone they are going to kill themselves. Verbal warnings should not be ignored.

MYTH: Talking to someone about suicide may increase the risk of them actually committing suicide.

FACT: The opposite is true. Asking someone if he or she feels suicidal or wants to kill himself or herself creates relief in the individual as well as opens a line of communication which can lead to help.

MYTH: If someone really wants to die, no one can stop him or her.

FACT: Most suicidal people are ambivalent about wanting to die. Many feel that they just want their emotional pain to stop, and they believe that death is the only avenue. They do not really want to die.

MYTH: There is a typical type of person who is most likely to commit suicide.

FACT: People of all ages and walks of life commit suicide. There is no "typical" type of suicidal person.

MYTH: Suicide often happens without warning.

FACT: Most people give warning signs. Sometimes these signs go unrecognized.

WHAT TO DO IF YOU SUSPECT A TEENAGER IS SUICIDAL

Trust your intuition.

If you **feel** a teenager may be suicidal then act as though your feelings are accurate.

Listen carefully.

Make sure they know that you are listening and trying to understand their feelings.

143

Tell them that you do not want them to commit suicide and how you and others would feel if they did.

🍎 Believe them.

If they tell you they want to die, let them know that you take them seriously.

🍎 Tell them you are deeply concerned.

Let them know you care and want to help.

🍎 Be direct.

Tell them that you do not want them to commit suicide and how you and others would feel if they did.

🍎 Ask them questions.

Find out if they have a plan for killing themselves, and if so, what exactly is their plan. Be aware that the more specific the plan, the greater the risk of suicide.

🍎 Make certain they do not have access to means of suicide.

Be sure they are not left with guns, pills or razors.

🍎 Get help.

Encourage the person to get professional help. Tell him or her that you will help tell his or her parents or counselors, but these people (especially the parents) must be told.

WHAT **NOT** TO DO IF YOU SUSPECT A TEENAGER IS SUICIDAL

🍎 Do not agree to keep the secret.

It is better to betray a confidence than lose a life.

🍎 Do not trust that they will be okay.

If they have told you that they have a specific plan or are committed to taking their own life, do not trust that they will be okay just because you have had a good talk.

🍎 Do not express your concern in the form of platitudes.

Be careful not to say things that sound trite and insincere, for example "You have so much to live for." Even if you believe this to be true, say it in a more personal way.

🍎 Do not leave the person alone.

If you believe the risk is high, do not trust their promise that they will be ok. Stay with them or get someone else to stay with them all the time until they are able to get the help they need.

🍎 Do not act shocked or judgmental.

Do not say, "How could you feel that way," or "You should count your blessings."

🍎 Do not debate whether suicide is right or wrong.

This could only make them feel worse. A debate of this nature appeals to their rational processes which are seriously impaired by their emotional pain.

🍎 Do not try to counsel them yourself.

Express your deep concern and encourage them to get professional help.

FINALLY...

Take care of yourself. Be aware of your own emotions when dealing with a suicidal adolescent. Give yourself permission to feel your own feelings (i.e., angry, scared, sad). Talk to a friend or colleague about your feelings. This is *essential* to your own well-being. Be kind to yourself.

RECOMMENDED READING

Barkley, Russell A. *Defiant Children: A Clinician's Manual for Parent Training.* New York, NY: The Guilford Press. 1987.

Divinyi, Joyce E. (1995) Storytelling: An Enjoyable and Effective Therapeutic Tool. (*Contemporary Famiy Therapy. An International Journal) 17, 27-37.ISSN:0892-2764.*

Dobson, James. *Hide or Seek.* Grand Rapids, MI: Ravell, 1974. ISBN-0-8007-5146-9

Faber, Adele and Mazlish, Elaine. *How To Talk So Kids Can Learn.* Simon & Schuster Audio Division, 1995. (Audio Cassette)

Ginott, Dr. Haim. *Between Parent and Child.* New York, NY: Avon Books, 1965.

Goleman, Daniel, Emotional Intelligence. New York, NY: 1995. Bantam Books ISBN-0-553-09503-X

Glenn, H. Stephen and Nelsen, Jane. *Raising Self-Reliant Children in a Self-Indulgent World.* Rocklin, CA: Prima Publishing and Communications, 1989. ISBN-0-914629-92-1

Glenn, H., Stephen and Nelsen, Jane. *Time Out—Abuses and Effective Uses.* Fair Oaks, CA: Sunrise Press, 1991. ISBN-0-9606896-8-0

Hartmann, Thom. *Attention Deficit Disorder: A Different Perception.* Lancaster, PA: Underwood-Miller, 1993. ISBN-0-88733-156-4

Kondracki, Linda. *Confident Kids: All My Feelings Are Okay.* Grand Rapids, MI: Fleming H. Revell (A Division of Baker Book House Co), 1993. ISBN-0-8007-5441-7

Koplewicz, Dr. Harold S. *It's Nobody's Fault.* New York, NY: Times Books, 1996. ISBN-0-8129-2473-8

Magid, Dr. Ken and McKelvey, Carole A. *High Risk Children Without a Conscience.* Golden, CO: M&M Publishing Co.,1987. ISBN-0-553-34667-9

Thompson, George J. and Jenkins, Jerry B. *Verbal Judo – The Gentle Art of Persuasion.* New York, NY: William Morrow and Company, Inc., 1993. ISBN-0-688-13786-5.

Tobin, L. *What Do You Do with a Child Like This?* Duluth, MN: Whole Person Associates, 1991. ISBN-0-938586-44-0

Tobin, L. *62 Ways to Create Change in the Lives of Troubled Children.* Duluth, MN: Whole Person Associates, 1991. ISBN-0-938586-47-5

Waliszewski, Bob and Melchisekeck, Jerry. *Bringing Out the Worst in Us,* Focus on the Family Culture Report. "The Frightening Truth About Violence, The Media and Our Youth." *To obtain a copy of this report you may call Focus On The Family at 1-800-A-FAMILY.*

All the *Calvin and Hobbs* books (to remind you to keep your sense of humor when dealing with difficult children...besides, Calvin has the CAN DO and I COUNT attitudes down pat).

Bring Successful Strategies to Your Organization

The Wellness Connection will provide specialized training programs for parents, schools or organizations serving children. Training programs are designed to facilitate and encourage the use of the highly effective communications and behavior management strategies outlined in "Successful Strategies for Working with Difficult Kids".

The Wellness Connection is a counseling and training company dedicated to helping children and adults live and work well together.

For Information About On-Site Training:

Joyce E. Divinyi, M.S.
Licensed Professional Counselor
The Wellness Connection
125 Highgreen Ridge
Peachtree City, GA 30269
(770) 631-8264
Toll-free Number: 1-888-460-8022
Fax: (770) 486-1609
E-mail Address: Divinyi@mindspring.com
Website: http://www.peachcity.com/wellness/
To Order the Book or Cassette Tapes Please Copy and Send/Fax to the above address.

Cassette Tapes:
"Safe and Effective Strategies for Defusing Hostile Students"
$10.00 plus $2.00 S&H.   Total: $12.00   Please send me _____ copy(ies)

"Successful Strategies for Dealing with Difficult Students"
$15.00 (2 tape set) plus $2.00 S&H. Total: $17.00   Please send me _____ copy(ies)

Book:
"Successful Strategies for Working (or Living) with Difficult Kids"
$19.95 plus $2.00 S&H.   Total: $21.95   Please send me _____ copy(ies)

Package:
All of the above—one book and two programs on cassettes.
$40.00 plus $2.00 S&H. Total: $42.00   Please send me _____ package(s)

Name _____

Organization Name _____

Address _____

City/State/Zip _____ County _____

Phone/Fax No. _____ Program Date _____

Method of Payment: ___ Visa ___ Master Card ___ Discover ___ Check ___ Bill Me
Make checks payable to: The Wellness Connection, 125 Highgreen Ridge, Peachtree City, GA 30269
or Fax: 770-486-1609 Phone: 770-631-8264 or 1-888-460-8022
Web-site: http://www.peachcity.com/wellness/
Email: divinyi@mindspring.com

Your Card Number: _____ Expiration Date: _____

Cardholder Signature: _____

QUANTITY DISCOUNTS AVAILABLE
1-9 Books ..... 19.95 ea.*   10-99 Books ..... 17.95 ea.*   100 Books or more ..... 14.95 ea.*
*Plus Shipping and Handling